The First-Time Forager

To Mum & Dad who gave their children the greatest gift to be bestowed on anyone – a wild garden to play in.

Andy Hamilton

The First-Time Forager

A complete beginner's guide to Britain's edible plants

Published by National Trust Books
An imprint of HarperCollins Publishers,
1 London Bridge Street
London SE1 9GF
www.harpercollins.co.uk

HarperCollins Publishers,
Macken House, 39/40 Mayor Street
Upper, Dublin 1, D01 C9W8,
Ireland

First published 2024

ISBN 978-0-00-864135-1
10 9 8 7 6 5 4 3 2 1

A catalogue record for this book is available from the British Library.

Printed and bound in India.

If you would like to comment on any aspect of this book,
please contact us at the above address or national.trust@harpercollins.co.uk

National Trust publications are available at National Trust shops or online at
nationaltrustbooks.co.uk

This book contains FSC™ certified paper and other controlled sources to ensure responsible forest management.

For more information visit: www.harpercollins.co.uk/green

Contents

Introduction

Have you ever picked a blackberry, an apple, a fig or any piece of fruit from a tree, vine or shrub? If you have, then you're a forager. I'd also bet that you can tell the difference between a blackberry, an apple and a fig. And you also probably know – just by looking at them – when they are past their best. These are the skills you need to be a forager, and you already have them.

We develop these skills of pattern recognition remarkably early. Under the watchful eyes of our parents, before we've even learnt to walk or speak, we start to recognise a variety of different fruits almost instinctively. I've recently been blessed with the opportunity to watch two small humans going through this very process. Both of my children can tell the difference between a plum and a grapefruit, and laugh at me if I ask them to differentiate between a banana and their granddad.

There are seven different wild edibles that most people know already: dandelions, nettles, apples, pears, blackberries, plums and raspberries. That's enough to have the taste of the wild on your plate all year round.

As you discover more, you'll have a whole array of skills at your disposal. You'll start to recognise and use plant families, seasonality, habitat and aroma to tell plants apart.

It's easy to assume that foraging is some kind of specialist activity. That it's the preserve of those who have an intimate knowledge of every plant and fungi around us. This is nonsense. Most foragers I have met – even those who've been teaching for years – will be flummoxed by the usages of some of the plants they encounter. You don't have to have a huge knowledge of the natural world to be a forager. You just have to know what is edible, and more importantly, what can make you ill.

Why don't we all eat wild plants?

Scientists at Kew Gardens estimate that there are in excess of 400,000 plants on the Earth; it's thought that over half of them could be edible. Yet we currently consume only around 200 of these plants.

This might sound like a decent number. That is, until you break it down: around half of our calorific intake comes from just three plants – maize, wheat and rice. The main reason for their success is not taste or nutritional content. Rather, it is because they're easy to grow. Farmed crops such as these only need a few gusts of wind to pollinate and thus reproduce.

In many ways, wild plants can outperform cultivated crops in terms of versatility, taste and nutrition. The reason we don't eat more of them is because they are often difficult to farm in sufficient quantities. However, if we all learned to forage, then perhaps we could be eating many more of these plants instead of relying on so much imported food.

How do you know which plants to eat?

What you want to know is which plants you can eat: how they look and taste, and where to find them. You'll also want to know if there are any dangerous plants that you might confuse with an edible plant, as well as any other associated dangers.

I hope that over the coming weeks, months and years, you'll get both inspiration and reassurance from this book. There is great joy in going for a walk in the morning and coming back with even just one piece of food to add to a lunch, a herb that can be made into a refreshing tea or the ingredients for your own wild gin. When foraging becomes part of your life, it develops into a skill that can be shared not just when out for a walk, but at mealtimes too.

At least 83 per cent of the population lives in a city, just as I do. This morning I left the house, went for a ten-minute walk and returned with all the food I needed for breakfast. I currently have friends in Manchester, Plymouth, Edinburgh, Leeds and London who all live off wild food for up to three months of the year.

This book will show you that driving out to woodland to forage is a misconception. I've found more diversity of wild food in the city than I ever have in the countryside. It's nice to get out and forage in the countryside, but you don't have to.

How much can I take?

Plants such as Japanese knotweed and three-cornered leek are considered invasive and therefore you can pick them to your heart's content. However, these are the exception rather than the rule.

Most of the plants in this book are relatively common. If you find one plant that is hosting a clutch of butterfly eggs, for example, then simply move on to another one. Likewise, if you find a plant growing on its own, leave it alone. Look for big patches of plants and then pick just a few of the leaves or some of the fruits. Some stick to the rule of 'count three and pick the third'. I try to count to ten.

Make sure to never pick the last seed head or more than you need. One of my foraging friends goes out into the woods with a shopping list. Although that might be a way off for the beginner, it's good practice to think about what meals you are going to make with the food you pick.

What if I make a mistake?

Stick to the idea that you need to be 100 per cent certain of anything you eat. Back this up with as many sources as you can: apps can be good, but personally I think botanical drawings, good photos and books are better. Also, you have to think about your approach to foraging. Be aware of where mistakes can happen. In my experience, I've found that two of the main reasons for poisoning include:

Bravado A little bit of knowledge can be a dangerous thing. I was out foraging with a chef once. In a show of boldness after a brief lesson, he picked some hemlock and then put it straight in his mouth. If it wasn't for the quick thinking of one of his staff, that chef's chain of restaurants would have been no more. Recognise and acknowledge doubt as a good thing. Being cautious can keep you alive. There is no shame in double-checking – even experienced foragers need to do so from time to time.

Making the plant fit the description You want to find wild garlic but instead you find an isolated plant that doesn't smell of garlic and has thick leaves. It's pretty close to the description, so why not pick it anyway? Never mind the fact that it could also be lords-and-ladies (*Arum maculatum*), a plant that may very well kill you. If you can avoid falling into these classic traps, you'll become a great forager.

Are there any other dangers?

There are, of course, other dangers out there, but as long as you are aware of them, they can be avoided too.

Look out for signs of contamination One of the first questions many people ask is 'What about dog wee?'

Well, often you'll see singe marks on plant leaves in the form of browning or blackening. These can be caused by dog wee, pesticides, insect damage, poor nutrients or the sun. As all the plants in this book can be found quite readily, simply avoid poor specimens and move on. Moreover, if picking close to somewhere dogs are walked is unavoidable, just wash your produce when you get it home, just as you would with shop-bought vegetables.

I would also avoid anything you suspect has been sprayed with pesticides. Although nothing is ever certain in science, the link between non-Hodgkin lymphoma and the leading pesticide sprays is becoming undeniable. You may become aware of a certain sweet smell in the air after pesticides have been sprayed. You'll also notice that the plants will have singe marks on the leaves. I tend to avoid picking right next to arable fields,

rose gardens and any overly neat park or garden when I'm out foraging. I suggest this is generally good practice.

There are fewer signs to look out for with land that has been contaminated by industry. There was a great mushroom spot near my old house. I later found out that it used to be owned by a chemical company and was once considered to be one of the most polluted places in Bristol. Rather than deal with the problem, they dumped loads of soil onto the land and declared it common ground.

If you are going to forage frequently in one or two spots, then do your homework. Avoid any site that was once home to heavy industry. Check with local history groups, look for laminated signs around the area and ask residents. Also, never pick next to motorways or close to sewers, and if you suspect that you've picked near an animal's den or livestock, then wash all food thoroughly.

Lastly, be respectful of footpaths, don't pick obvious crops, avoid trespassing and never excavate a root without the landowner's permission.

What about the law and common sense?

There are a few bits of law every forager needs to be aware of. First, there is Section 4 (Property) of the Theft Act (1968) (England and Wales only, though it's similar in Scotland) where the following applies: 'A person who picks mushrooms growing wild on any land, or who picks flowers, fruit or foliage from a plant growing wild on any land, does not (although not in possession of the land) steal what he picks, unless he does it for reward or for sale or other commercial purpose.'

Note the last part in particular: the chances of being arrested for picking blackberries, turning them into jam and then selling them on at a church fête are remote. However, if you develop branding and start selling your products to shops, then you could find yourself in hot water.

The next piece of the law you need to think about relates to trespass. You'll see that some of the plants in this book grow in parks and gardens. In England, you need the landowner's permission to go onto their private land and forage. Although picking plants like nettles will stimulate new growth, and evidence is mounting to say that mushroom picking does the same, some landowners still do not allow foraging on their land.

Use common sense in all cases. Farms are private property but they can be zig-zagged using public footpaths and minor roads. These are generally considered fair game as long as you observe the Countryside Act, and don't go pulling up or trampling on crops, or veering too far from marked paths. The National Trust supports sustainable foraging at many of its places, though it's not permitted at protected sites, including nature reserves and Sites of Special Scientific Interest (SSSI), so it's always best to check before you visit.

There are also some plants that are protected and thus illegal to pick. A full list can be found by searching for Schedule 8 of the Wildlife and Countryside Act (1981).

Be respectful

The overall take-home from all this is to be respectful. Think about whether you'd like to find someone picking from the apple tree in your front garden. You might be okay about kids taking one or two apples (or you might not), but if they stripped the tree and broke some of the branches you'd be justifiably annoyed. What then if someone came right up to your front window and started foraging in your window boxes while you were eating breakfast. Farms and stately homes are often places where other fellow humans live, so treat them as you would treat your friends and family.

The plants

Over the past two decades I've foraged on islands as well as in cities, towns, suburbs, villages, woods, beaches, grasslands, parks, car parks, river and canal sides and gardens. The plants in this book are all fairly common, especially around human habitation, which hopefully means your home. I've even included plants that you may find in your own garden (if you're lucky enough to have one) or at the local park.

My aim is that you'll find this book useful and informative, but more than that, I hope that it opens up a world of taste for you and your family and friends.

A short Latin lesson

It's easy to be intimidated by the Latin names you'll come across here – I know I was at first. Over the years, I've come to embrace it. Think of it like a coding language such as CSS or HTML: languages that enable computers to talk to each other, no matter which operating system they use, or which country they are in. These common computer languages ensure the functioning of the internet. In a similar way, Latin is the language used across cultures and countries to talk about the natural world: animals, fungi and plants all have Latin names.

Back in the sixteenth century, plants were known either by a long, highly descriptive sentence or by a common name. However, common names can be problematic as they are often used for more than one plant: goosegrass, for example, is used for at least nine different species. Then there are common plants such as *Galium aparine*, which is also known as cleavers, sticky willy, stick weed, sticky bobs, sticky back, robin-run-the-hedge, catchweed, bobby buttons, goosegrass, gollenweed, sweethearts, kisses and claggy meggies. With that many names, how can botanists across the world know they are talking about the same plant?

When the printing press began to shape the way information was shared, a streamlined process was needed to save any confusion. Along came Swiss botanist Caspar Bauhin, who in the early 1600s started using two names for each plant, a process further refined by Swedish naturalist Carl Linnæus in the eighteenth century. Linnæus took it upon himself to classify the whole natural world, giving everything a group name (or surname) and a first name. His system of using a genus and species name derived from Latin to give a unique name to each individual species became the basis of plant classification.

Think of it like this, I'm called Andy Hamilton. My surname or genus is Hamilton and my first name or species is Andy. In the plant world the genus comes first, so the wild rose or dog rose is known as *Rosa canina*, the Japanese rose has the name *Rosa rugosa* and sweet briar is called *Rosa rubiginosa*.

You'll notice that some plants have the letters 'spp.' next to them. This is an abbreviation that means more than one species, and botanists use this when grouping plants together. So, if I want to talk about roses in general, I can write *Rosa* spp. instead of listing the hundreds of different varieties of closely related roses. If you can become more familiar with this system, then not only are you a forager, but you are something of a botanist too.

APPLE

The leaves have serrated edges.

Fruit can vary in colour from green, yellow, orange, red to deep purple. If you cut one in half horizontally, you should see a five-pointed star of pips.

Blossom can be white or pink.

The scaly, greyish bark becomes cracked with age.

Apple

Malus spp.

Varying my diet is one of the main reasons I forage. The apple typifies this – every single pip will grow a genetically different tree; every crab or wild apple has the potential to taste wildly different than the next.

Many people write off the crab apple as an astringent and sour fruit. The forager knows different. Granted, many of the fruits are, but then you find the elusive and magical ones, those that are just delicious, tiny, highly unique apples. Often these are the ones that hang about over winter, developing sugars which make them even tastier.

Apples are a wild food that can be identified with help from a shop. Nip to your greengrocer and buy some apples. Cut one in half so you slice through just above the apple's equatorial line. You should be presented with a neat, five-pointed star shape. Next, study the size and shape of the pips inside. You may already know what apple pips look like, but have you ever studied them with intent? Look at the tear-drop shape, how each one slightly differs in colour and form. The apples you find in the wild will look just like this.

AT A GLANCE

Where they grow

Woodland where there is enough light; roadsides; abandoned gardens.

Brief description

Gobstopper-sized fruits, varying in size up to an American baseball.

Lookalikes

Whitebeam fruits (also edible but not in quantity).

Dangers

Falling apples; apple allergy.

Conservation notes

Be careful not to damage older trees with vigorous shaking or by climbing on weak branches.

When to harvest

September until late winter.

Use in

Eat raw; dehydrated rings; wine; pies; chutneys.

Fun fact

King Henry VIII loved apples. His orchard of mostly French grafted trees in Teynham, Kent, became the foundation for Britain's wide variety of apples.

The leaves have serrated edges and can be hairy. The blossoms range in colour from white to pink. They also vary in the time that they flower, but generally they are later than the plums and cherries, often appearing around late spring. Trees come in a great variety of sizes and shapes, from small, shrub-like ones, right up to beauties that are about 15 metres (50 feet) tall.

London-based forager, John Rensten, first introduced me to dehydrated crab apples – a delicious snack. The dehydration process sweetens the fruit. Simply cut into thin slices and pop into a low oven or dehydrator until crisp. Alternatively, you don't have to totally dehydrate them, and can slow roast instead. Forager Liz Knight recommends two hours in an oven at 100°C /80°C fan/200°F/gas ¼, with a coating of sugar and ground cinnamon, all wrapped up in a parcel of baking paper.

Simple crab apple mead

I sometimes wonder if this recipe was one of the first ever alcoholic drinks. I imagine an ancient beehive sitting in the hollow of a crab apple tree. The fallen hive mingles with the dropped fruit and the wild yeasts get to work. A week or two later, a hungry protohuman scoops up the resulting boozy broth and experiences a pleasant light-headedness.

Ingredients

A jar full of crab apples
Raw honey

Method

Cut your crab apples in half and drop them into a clean jar. Any apples or crab apples will do as long as they are wild. Top up with honey, leaving a small gap at the top. Cover with a small piece of cloth and seal with an elastic band (this keeps out flies). Leave out of direct sunlight to ferment for 2-3 weeks.

Filter and serve.

You can water the liquid down a little and drink it, but it also works neat as a base for a cocktail.

The bee's pyjamas

Inspiration for this cocktail came from the classic Tom Collins. I used the mead in place of the usual sugar syrup. If your mead is overly dry, I'd suggest using a teaspoon of honey to balance it.

Ingredients

50ml/2fl oz gin
30ml/2 tablespoons crab apple mead
30ml/2 tablespoons lemon juice
Sprig of ground ivy or thyme

Method

Pour the gin, mead, lemon juice and two cubes of ice into a cocktail shaker. Shake well and strain into a champagne glass with a sprig of ground ivy or thyme. Some like to top up with soda water but I prefer it neat.

BEECH

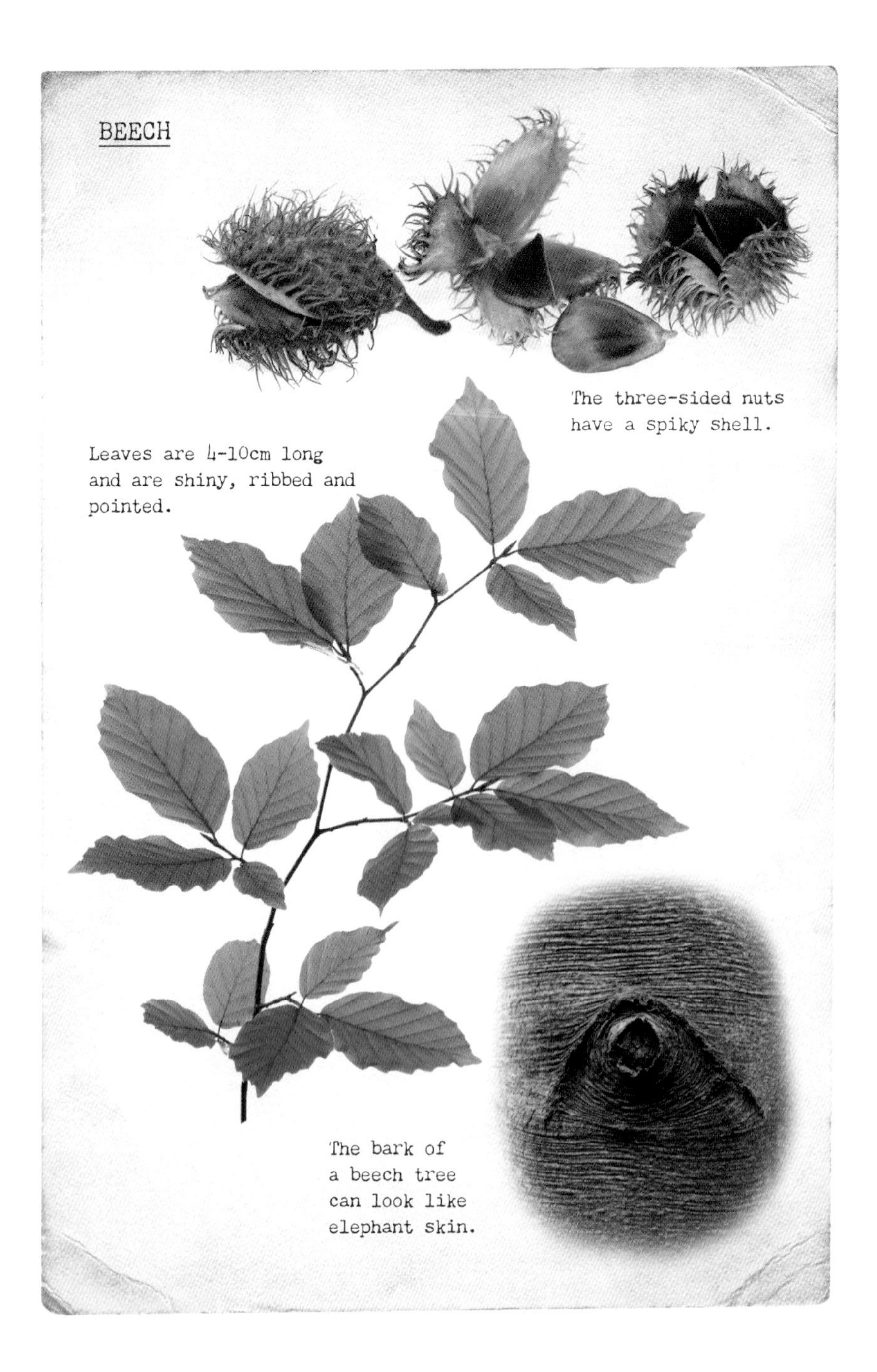

The three-sided nuts have a spiky shell.

Leaves are 4-10cm long and are shiny, ribbed and pointed.

The bark of a beech tree can look like elephant skin.

Beech

Fagus spp.

The majestic beech is easy to spot from a distance due to its size, growing to the height of around 40 metres (130 feet) or four double-decker buses. It supports a massive, rounded canopy; a mature specimen has branches that spread out almost as wide as it is tall. You'll also notice that its great grey trunk resembles an elephant's leg.

When the twigs start to bud in the spring, you'll find spear-like buds protected by a tiny shield that is shed as they grow, littering the ground. These tightly wound little parcels will soon become the leaves, which are ovate (sort of egg shaped). They are about 4–10 centimetres (1.5–4 inches) long and are shiny, ribbed and pointed. The younger leaves are often light green with hairs on the side.

You might also note how the roots spread out from the base, creating what look like rock pools that fill with water around the bottom of the tree. If you don't notice this, your thirsty dog will.

While your dog is busy slaking its thirst, search around the base of the tree. Look for beech nuts and leaves; as they are among the

AT A GLANCE

Where they grow

Anywhere from dense woodland and hedgerows to parks and gardens.

Brief description

Trunk resembles the skin of an elephant; large canopy.

Lookalikes

Oaks, hornbeam and other large trees.

Dangers

Nuts need to be roasted and shouldn't be eaten in large quantities.

Conservation notes

Don't strip all the leaves from a tree.

When to harvest

Fresh leaves in spring; dried leaves and nuts in autumn.

Use in

Leaves can be fried.

Fun fact

The Meikleour Beech hedge in Scotland is the highest in the world at 30m (100ft) tall. It was a tribute to the men who planted it, as they all lost their lives in the Jacobite rebellion of 1745.

last leaves to fall, there are often both beneath a beech. The shells are spiky and contain roughly triangular, three-sided nuts.

A few people react badly to the nuts, therefore it is a good idea to roast them – which has the bonus of making them tastier too! To prepare, remove the nuts from the shell: score down the husk, remove the inner nut and toast in a frying pan.

Beech leaves can remain on the tree throughout the winter. Used sparingly, and not by anyone with kidney problems, the naturally dry leaves can be made into a tea. Simply pick a few and infuse in hot water.

Beech leaf crisps

The nuts can be rather fiddly to extract. It's far easier to harvest the leaves. Pick them in the spring when they are still light green and translucent. I move from branch to branch and pull them straight off, but only a few at a time, never stripping the tree, and avoiding harvesting altogether from younger, small and thin trees.

Ingredients

A good couple of handfuls of beech leaves
30ml/2 tablespoons of oil

Method

Heat up the oil in a pan until it is bubbling. Fry the leaves in batches until they are crispy. Place onto kitchen roll.

Serve warm and add a little salt to taste.

Blackberry

Rubus fruticosus agg.

Blackberries are a simple and delicious wild food source that takes seconds to learn about and offers a lifetime of nutritious delight. Part of their success in colonising everywhere is because there are many different varieties of bramble – the name for the shrub they grow on. A floral survey of the Bristol area names almost a hundred, less than a third of all the known microspecies.

Practically, this means that when picking the fruit you'll find some full of seeds, some that are hard and perhaps a little too tart, some small but delicious and others which are fat, juicy and delectable. We have varieties that match each of these descriptions near where I live. Some we save for wines, jams and puddings, some are popped into whisky as an infusion and others are simply washed and eaten whole.

The flowers are white or pink and bloom from May to September. The berries start off small and are hard and green; as they ripen they turn red and then black, softening as they go.

The leaves are extremely good as a tea: the Scottish poet, Robert Burns, was thought

AT A GLANCE

Where they grow

Anywhere that is undisturbed

Brief description

Grow in groups on thorny vines. Berries ripen from green through to red then black.

Lookalikes

Dewberries – also edible.

Dangers

Be careful of the thorns. The leaves often have spikes on the underside too, which can give you a nasty cut.

When to harvest

Leaves spring–summer; fruit in late summer and early autumn; shoots in later winter.

Use in

Pies and puddings; wines and as an alcoholic infusion; eat raw or mix into a smoothie.

Fun fact

A country name for brambles used to be 'lawyers', as once they get hold of you it is difficult to break loose.

BLACKBERRY

The thorns have yet to harden on this edible new shoot.

The small, five-petalled flowers are white or pink.

Berries on a vine, from unripe green to ripe and almost black.

to enjoy them as part of a moorland tea mix. They can be simply air-dried, along with equal parts of heather, wild strawberry, bilberry leaf and thyme; some people mix them in with regular tea leaves. Another variation is to ferment the blackberry leaves. Crushed and pounded, they can be packed tightly into a sterile jar and then left for 2–6 weeks. They will turn black. Don't be afraid of the white mould that will grow on them, it's part of the process; simply rub this off and dry out your leaves either in a low oven or a dehydrator.

The pale green blackberry shoots can also be eaten. These are the first shoots of the leaves growing on the previous year's vines or out of the ground. Harvest from late February to early summer, before they have a chance to harden up, and while the sugar levels are still high. They can be eaten straight off the plant and make a great wayside snack. As the season progresses you can still harvest longer, spikier shoots. These will need to be peeled before eating. Make sure to leave some shoots on the shrub, otherwise there won't be many blackberries come autumn.

Blackberry sidecar

Blackberries are excellent when used in drinks, blackberry wine being an absolute favourite. However, if you are wanting something a little more complex, sophisticated and moreish I assure you that this twist on a traditional sidecar cocktail will not disappoint.

Ingredients

6-10 blackberries
30ml/2 tablespoons blackberry-infused apple brandy
15ml/1 tablespoon Cointreau
5ml/1 teaspoon sugar syrup
15ml/1 tablespoon lemon juice, freshly squeezed
Apple slice to serve

Method

Gently crush the berries in the bottom of a shaker. Add ice, followed by the other ingredients.

Shake until your hand is cold. Strain into a large cocktail glass and garnish with a thin slice of apple.

Blackberry fool

Classic fool recipes were made by folding fruit into custard. These days, recipes have become much simpler, and this one is no exception.

Ingredients

500g/1lb 2oz blackberries
150g/5½oz caster sugar
Juice of half a lemon
400ml/14fl oz double cream
3 drops vanilla essence

Method

Push the blackberries through a sieve and combine the resulting juice and pulp with the sugar in a bowl. Squeeze in the lemon juice.

In a separate bowl whisk the double cream until thick, adding the vanilla essence. Fold the contents of the bowls together. Pop in the fridge to chill for an hour or so before serving.

Devilled blackberry

This recipe came via the Midlands most highly respected wild food chefs, Alexander McAllister-Lunt. I swear that five minutes in his company is like a month in chef school. This recipe uses frozen blackberries, something foragers can often find in the back of their freezers.

Ingredients

1 heaped tablespoon of Gunpowder mustard
200g/7oz blackberries (frozen from last season)
5-10 fresh horseradish leaves (depending on size)
50g/1¾oz young mugwort leaves (or ground ivy or wild garlic)
25g/1oz green hogweed seeds
100g/3½oz Parma ham or 200g/7oz smoked streaky bacon
Smoked sea salt flakes and wild (or raw) honey

Method

Spread out the heaped tablespoon of Gunpowder mustard on a plate and place the blackberries on top. Roll them around or use a spoon to ensure a good coating (the blackberries can still be partially frozen at this point).

Cut down either side of the horseradish leaf stem to remove the leaves, tear the mugwort and remove the stalks from the hogweed seeds.

Lay a slice of Parma ham out on a chopping board, arrange the leaves and seeds on top and then spoon a blackberry or two on one side and roll tightly, folding in the sides as you go. Repeat and set aside until you are ready to cook (you can prep the night before).

When ready to cook, pre-heat your grill to high and place the parcels on a baking tray, keep an eye on them and turn as required to get a nice golden brown, crispy finish.

I like to garnish with more mugwort, hogweed seeds, smoked Cornish sea salt and a little drizzle of wild honey.

CHERRY

The beautiful spring blossom is short-lived and can be any shade of pink to white.

Look for the all-important single cherry pip.

The bark has horizontal bands.

Bird cherry has pea-sized fruit.

Cherry

Prunus spp.

Followers of Japanese Shinto (神道) do not separate humankind from nature. They believe that nature is sacred, and we should live in harmony with it. The short-lived blossom of cherry trees encapsulates the ephemeral nature of human life. In other words, cherry blossom reminds us that life is short, precious and utterly beautiful.

Come June and July, the blossom has turned into fruit that is equally precious and beautiful but also ripe and tasty. Wild cherry trees can grow up to 30 metres (100 feet) tall and so picking the fruit from a mature tree can be a challenge. Ingenuity can overcome this hurdle. Ladders are used by fruit farmers who know the terrain, but if you want to keep your feet firmly on the ground then perhaps invest in a cherry-picking tool. These are essentially little bags on an extendable rod. They take a bit of getting used to but can increase the harvest.

In order to identify a cherry tree, hone in on the bark first. Check for horizontal bands across the trunk. Known as lenticels, these help the tree breathe in winter. More mature trees will also have vertical splits in the bark.

AT A GLANCE

Where they grow

Parks; gardens; verges; townscapes where a flash of optimism is needed.

Brief description

Pea-sized to marble-sized fruit. Colour ranges from yellow to deep, dark ox-blood red – almost black.

Lookalikes

Edible: service berry, crab apple. Poisonous: red bryony; Christmas cherry; cherry laurel.

Dangers

The bird cherry contains higher levels of hydrogen cyanide, so do not eat too many.

When to harvest

June–July.

Use in

Pies; cherry brandy; can be eaten raw.

Fun fact

Up until the 1960s an old law in Kansas, USA, stated that serving ice cream on cherry pie was prohibited.

To identify the tree further, check the fruit by splitting one open. Look for the all-important single cherry pip. Fruits will vary in size depending on the type of cherry, from large, fat morello cherries to tiny wild cherries. Cherry laurel is an evergreen with shiny, bright green leaves but poisonous berries. It's easy to tell cherry trees and laurel apart but mistakes can be made. Always check thoroughly before eating.

Cherries grow from a long cherry stalk (pedicel); edible cherries grow in pairs and are often a bright red. The bitter bird cherry (*Prunus padus*) grows along a stem in a bunch – like tiny grapes – and is almost black when ripe.

The wild cherry (*Prunus avium*) is native across much of the temperate Northern Hemisphere, from America to Japan. Often, however, it's the introduced and cultivated ones that are most prized. I've found the sweet, black cultivated cherry in parks and abandoned gardens and wild cherries close to allotments or on the edges of woodland and clearings.

Fruits can vary in taste from sweet to bitter and the latter are best reserved for jams or pies. With its pea-sized fruit, the bird cherry tends to be found near water or in sparse wooded areas. The fruits can be bitter and are best when cooked.

The bitterness derives from a glycoside called amygdalin. It releases hydrogen cyanide when the fruit is crushed and is present in the pips and leaves. This might sound worrying. After all, cyanide is most certainly poisonous. However, right up until the 1940s, the hunter-gatherer communities of the Amur Valley in Russia ate them as a staple food throughout the winter months. They pounded the whole fruit, flattened them out into little patties, and then roasted them until the almond-like flavour, and thus the poison, had gone.

Chickweed

Stellaria media

Chickweed was the first plant I fell in love with. I came across it when it had made itself at home between the ditches we had dug for childhood games. After a period away, the chickweed had sprung up as if by magic. This magnificent plant danced slightly in the wind, spot-lit by the dappled light shining through the pine trees at the wild end of our garden.

By digging trenches, overturning the soil, I'd created the ideal conditions for this ubiquitous plant. It loves to inhabit disturbed ground and can be found in most places where the land is cultivated, such as field edges, allotments and well-tended gardens. It also likes shady damp spots such as the edges of walls and beneath tree cover on forest edges and clearings. It's found in all but the driest of months and should be easy to locate as it is thought to be one of the most common plants in Britain.

The tiny white flowers carry five V-shaped petals, giving the impression that there are ten of them. One of chickweed's key characteristics is the fine hair that grows up the stem. This is key to its success, as these hairs trap dew and

AT A GLANCE

Where they grow

In moist, shady and cool places – e.g. beneath trees, against walls. Also likes disturbed/cultivated nutrient-rich ground.

Brief description

A low-growing plant, no more than 4cm/2in high in most gardens; sub-species can reach up to 50cm/1½ft. Found in clumps, often over a piece of dug-over ground. Opposite leaves; small white flowers. A single line of hair leads to each joint, visible under bright light.

Lookalikes

Stitchworts; mouse-ears; scarlet and yellow pimpernels.

Dangers

Confusion with pimpernels (see main text).

When to harvest

All year; scarce in hot summers.

Fun fact

Chickweed is currently being tested for a range of ailments, from diabetes to inflammation.

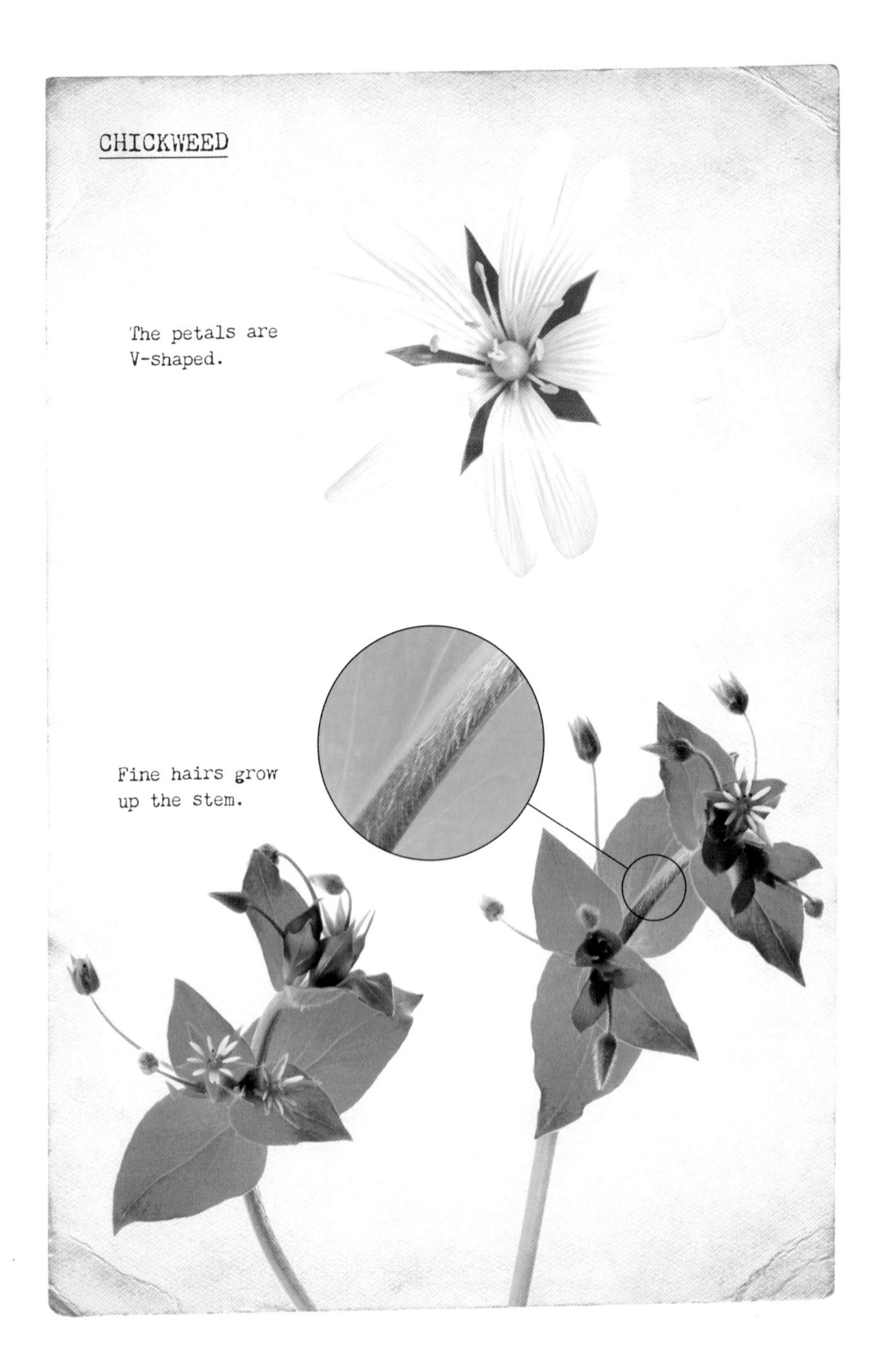
CHICKWEED
The petals are V-shaped.
Fine hairs grow up the stem.

moisture and direct it down the grooved stem of the leaves. This tiny reserve of water helps to hydrate this moisture-loving plant during dry weather.

Each plant can produce over a thousand viable seeds and it is capable of producing five generations of growth every year. This translates to a harvest that lasts most of the year, barring the hottest summer months. Gardeners might hate it, but it's easy to pull up and is one of the tastiest of the salad crops.

Chickweed has a fresh and earthy taste, which means it has the power to lift a simple recipe. Some call it a wild 'micro green'. It certainly can be used to give salads a boost. Cut off the top leaves and leave the stringy bottom section. I add mine, chopped up, to sushi rolls or pea soup. I've seen chefs add chickweed to a bowl of warm seasonal vegetables; it wilts down to nothing but provides an additional layer of flavour.

Chickweed can be one of the few plants you'll find growing in the winter months. It contains as much iron as spinach and is packed with nutrients and minerals and so is well worth braving the cold weather for.

It does look remarkably like scarlet pimpernel (*Anagallis arvensis*) and yellow pimpernel (*Lysimachia nemorum*). The way to differentiate chickweed from the pimpernels is that the latter lack a hairy stem. This might not be enough for the most cautious of people, so check the leaves. If none are connected to the main stem via a petiole (leaf stalk), you'll be okay. Also, look at the shape of the flowers, as both yellow and scarlet pimpernel have five pointed petals, rather than the five V-shaped petals of chickweed.

Dandelion

Taraxacum spp.

My daughter used to call these 'daddylions'. I'd like to think it was because she saw me picking and eating the leaves, but it may just have been a (very cute) three-year-old's mistaken pronunciation.

Although I might advocate nibbling on the raw leaves, they are very bitter. However, using them as a delicious variation of the Greek dish *horta vrasta* often leads to appreciative arched eyebrows when served as a side dish. It helps bring out a light, fragrant flavour with a hint of aniseed.

There a few different ways to make this simple dish, which roughly translates to 'boiled greens'. You can use any variety of wild or cultivated greens, such as mallow, good King Henry, chicory, sow thistle, chard, nettles and sorrel. Mixing and matching just as you might with a salad. I like to make the following dish just with dandelion leaves.

Simply wash the leaves to remove any dirt or grit. Bring to the boil and simmer for about 20 minutes. Drain and serve with a drizzle of olive oil, salt and lemon juice. Alternatively, you can warm 200ml (7fl oz)

AT A GLANCE

Where they grow

Most kinds of habitat: allotments, lawns, meadows and woodland clearings.

Brief description

Jagged leaves, pom-pom-like bright yellow flowers.

Lookalikes

The leaves grow in a similar rosette to ragwort (see page 172). Other members of the Asteraceae family, but these are also edible.

Dangers

Leaf sap can cause dermatitis in those who are susceptible.

When to harvest

Flowers, April; roots, autumn/spring; leaves, year round.

Use in

Drinks, salads and as a side dish. All parts of the plant are edible.

Fun fact

The word 'dandelion' derives from the French *dent-de-lion* or 'lion's tooth'. Yet in France it is known as *pissenlit* or 'wet the bed' due to its diuretic qualities.

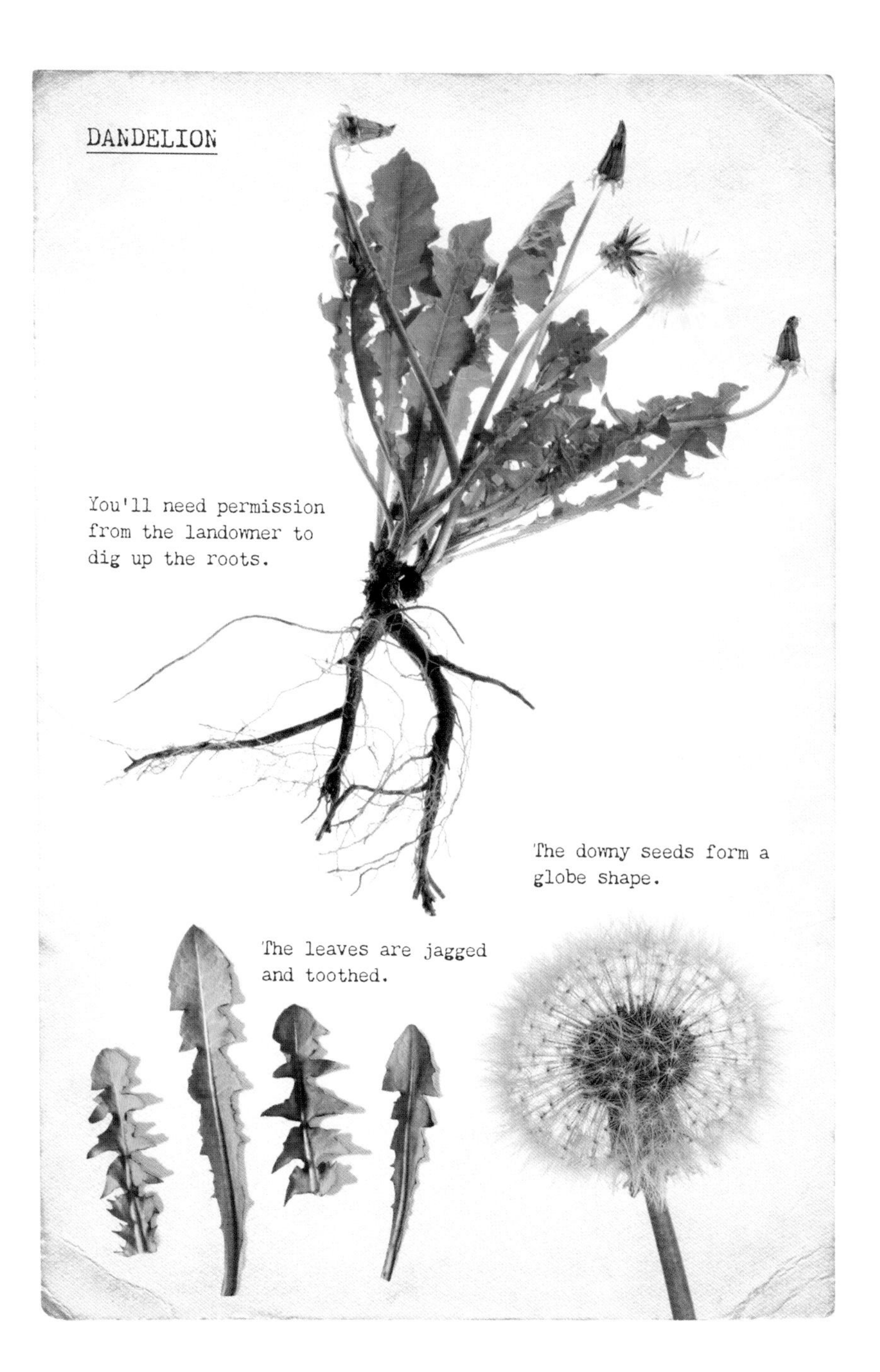
DANDELION
You'll need permission from the landowner to dig up the roots.
The downy seeds form a globe shape.
The leaves are jagged and toothed.

of full fat milk and crumble in 300g (10oz) of feta. Whizz in a blender and serve over the top – heaven!

With the landowner's permission, the roots can also be dug up. These are also tinged with the characteristic bitterness, and yes, you can wash them down then nibble on them raw. However, I like to boil them, until they take a fork easily, and then I gently fry them in butter – which always makes everything taste wonderful. Along with lashings of soy sauce, and maybe a sprinkling of sesame seeds, they top off a simple ramen dish.

You can also roast them: pop in the oven until they are dark, and then grind to make a coffee, approximately 1 tablespoon of powdered root per cup. Fellow forager and friend John Wright first suggests making a dandelion root latte, which he describes as 'good enough'. High praise indeed from this mild-mannered man.

When selecting your roots, you should go for freshly grown roots; old ones are thick and woody and don't make for good eating. But how can you tell which are past their prime? Well, the leaves look weathered, they are darker green than younger plants and are thicker too. Instead look for fresh, thin, pale green leaves.

Dandelions should be easy enough to spot as they grow almost everywhere. Towards the end of April, almost exactly on St George's Day, you'll find them in flower. Choose the right spot and you'll find whole fields painted yellow with their blooms. The leaves can be found and picked all year round and used, battered and fried, in salads, wine or as a vegan honey.

Dandelion honey

To make this honey, pluck out the petals from about 200 dandelions (they weigh roughly a gram each). You may want to enlist the help of children, perhaps with bribery, for this task, but don't pick all the dandelions in one place, even if there are plenty. Go for a walk and slowly fill a small bag. You'll have a nicer morning and the bees will still be able to gather their nectar.

Ingredients

115g/4oz dandelion heads
1 lemon/2 sprigs spruce/
 1 fistful pine needles
550ml/20fl oz water
500g/1lb 2oz sugar

Method

Wash and then leave the dandelions on the kitchen side for an hour or so; this will allow any small insects to escape.

Remove the petals from the calyx (the green bit below the petals). You can either snip them off with scissors or firmly grab the petals in one hand. Soak the petals for 10 mins and drain before putting in a saucepan.

Add a small lemon, sliced, or two sprigs from a fragrant spruce or a fistful of pine needles and the water. Bring to a boil and then simmer for 20 mins. Leave to infuse overnight.

Strain out the petals and compost them, keeping the flavoured dandelion water. Add equal the volume of liquid in sugar. Boil for up to an hour, checking every 10 mins. It helps to do the plate test here. Put a plate in the freezer for 10 mins. Take it out and dollop the honey on the plate; if it feels viscous and thick, the consistency of honey, it is done.

Transfer the honey into jars and keep as you would regular honey. It may crystallise with age, but you can warm the jars in a bain-marie to return it to runny honey.

ELDER
The clusters of frothy
flowers come in different
sizes.
The spear-shaped leaves
have jagged edges.
The clusters of small, round
black/purple fruits droop
downwards.

Elder

Sambucus nigra

I once met a druid who told me that the elder trees in a certain part of Bristol were all grumpy so-and-sos. It may seem like an unusual remark, but this is part of an ancient tradition.

There is a custom that goes back many generations where you must ask permission from the tree spirit before picking from any elder tree. She is an ancient vegetation Goddess named Hylde Moer, or 'elder mother', who is thought to watch over all the elder trees, avenging any injury done to her offspring. Furniture makers would find their creations haunted, cots would rock themselves or babies would find themselves swapped for faeries.

Rather conveniently, if Hylde Moer was going to allow you to take her wood, she would consent by staying silent. Whether or not you believe in these folk tales, there are often nuggets of practical information hidden within them. Every part of the elder tree is poisonous apart from the blossom and the cooked fruits. Perhaps the story of the curse is really a warning about the potential for poisoning.

AT A GLANCE

Where they grow

Hedgerows; field edges; parks and gardens.

Brief description

Small, straggly tree with beautiful, white scented blossoms.

Lookalikes

Carrot family and guelder rose.

Dangers

Uncooked berries; elder wood; confusion with hemlock (see main text).

When to harvest

Flowers in early summer; berries in late summer.

Use in

Flowers in cordials; fritters; gin; tea. Berries in wine; desserts.

Fun fact

Elderberries are great for making countryside wines and have been called the 'Englishman's grape'.

I sometimes wonder just how many cursed people there are out there, considering that there is no other wild food that is sold to us in greater abundance than the elder. Soft drinks containing elderflower, flavoured tonic water, herbal teas, spirits, cough syrups and cordials can all be bought in supermarkets. Did all these pickers ask the tree spirits for permission?

One thing I've observed about novice foragers is that they tend to get excited about elderflower and want to see it everywhere. It's perfectly natural, but it can be quite dangerous. I've been sent photos of plants from the carrot family, a family that contains hemlock, and had more than one person say, 'We thought it was ground elder as it was growing on the ground'. This is an easy mistake to make when starting out, as the leaves are a similar spear-shape and also have jagged edges. But the elder tree is a shrub, not a herbaceous plant.

The surest way to identify elderflowers is by the smell. If you are unfamiliar with it, head down to your local pub and order a glass of elderflower pressé and give it a good sniff. Or nip to your local supermarket and buy a bottle of elderflower cordial. However, when the heady scents of the pollen have gone and after heavy rain, the leaves and the flowers can give off a horrible smell akin to cat pee. As the summer draws to a close, the berries will ripen, weighing down the clusters with their small, round purple-black fruits.

I drink elderflower tea in hay fever season as a preventative and whenever I feel a cold coming on. Put 1 teaspoon of fresh or half a teaspoon of dried elderflowers in a mug and pour over boiling water. Leave to infuse for 3–5 minutes. Strain and drink when needed, at a rate of around three cups a day.

Evening primrose

Oenothera spp.

Evening primrose might be an American import, but this biennial (a plant that grows over two years) has successfully naturalised across the UK. There are confirmed sightings from the shores of the Cromarty Firth in Scotland right down to the Isle of Wight.

A few plants can turn into many, and it tends to creep out of gardens and allotments, especially in sunny conditions and on poor soil. You can notice it growing from May to December. As last year's skeletons remain standing, they work as a marker telling you where to harvest the next year's leaves, while also offering a home to countless insects. Once you know what you are looking for, you can return to the same spot each year.

In its first year, evening primrose forms a rosette of leaves at the base, which grows to about 5 centimetres (2 inches) in diameter. In the second year, leaves form a spiral up the stem, which can grow up to 1.5 metres (5 feet) high. The vast majority of plants will have a single stem; very occasionally they will branch off.

AT A GLANCE

Where they grow

Sandy soils with plenty of sun.

Brief description

Pretty, tall flower with many vivid yellow flower heads.

Lookalikes

Other varieties of evening primrose.

Dangers

Can interact with some medications. Consult a medical professional if you're on regular medication or have an underlying health condition.

Conservation notes

Leave whole plants standing after harvesting. It will benefit the insects.

When to harvest

Summer–autumn.

Use in

Salads; stews; curries.

Fun fact

The Anishinaabe peoples of North America traditionally make tea from evening primrose leaves to reduce fatigue.

EVENING PRIMROSE

The long, lance-shaped leaves grow in a spiral up the stem.

Buds appear from late spring onwards; these turn into bright yellow flowers.

Buds will appear from late spring onwards, and these turn into bright yellow flowers. In its second year, the plant will grow many flowers on the upper 60 centimetres (2 feet) of the stem. I like to snack on both the buds and flowers as I wander past my local thicket.

All parts of this plant are edible. I use the buds in place of fried onions in soups and curries, adding a peppery flavour, and the leaves (sparingly) in salads. The roots (dug up with permission of the landowner) are sublime par-boiled and served with cream and a bit of grated Cheddar.

Fennel

Foeniculum vulgare

I'm always delighted when I see the feathery shaped, very finely branched leaves of fennel waving away at me from a distance. They somehow seem to beckon me over, urging me to pick them.

Depending on your experience, you may want to be a little cautious when identifying fennel. It does belong to the carrot family after all, but you can use shops to help you. Buy a few fennel seeds and then crush them in your hands. Give them a smell and familiarise yourself with this key characteristic.

Now check the central stem, does it remind you of the Florence fennel stem you see growing out of a shop-bought bulb? It has fairly thick and robust grooves, the leaves slightly feathery, and it looks a lot like dill. If you don't know what dill looks like, but have a local Eastern European deli or a decent-sized supermarket, then pop in as they often stock some. It has distinctive bright yellow flowers, which are shaped like an upside-down umbrella. You may confuse these with wild parsnip, just check for the feathery leaves and the smell.

AT A GLANCE

Where they grow

Often coastal but can spread inland; rarer in the North.

Brief description

Up to 2m/6½ft tall. Feathery, finely branched leaves. Smells of fennel/aniseed.

Lookalikes

Wild parsnip; dill; cow parsnip when in flower.

Dangers

Confusing it with wild parsnip as the sap from this plant can burn skin in sunlight, or with other potentially harmful members of the carrot family, such as giant hogweed.

When to harvest

Leaves in spring/summer; seeds in autumn.

Use in

Leaves in salads; seeds to flavour dishes.

Fun fact

Fennel appears in the earliest English recipe for salad. This dates back to 1390 and was compiled by the cooks of Richard II.

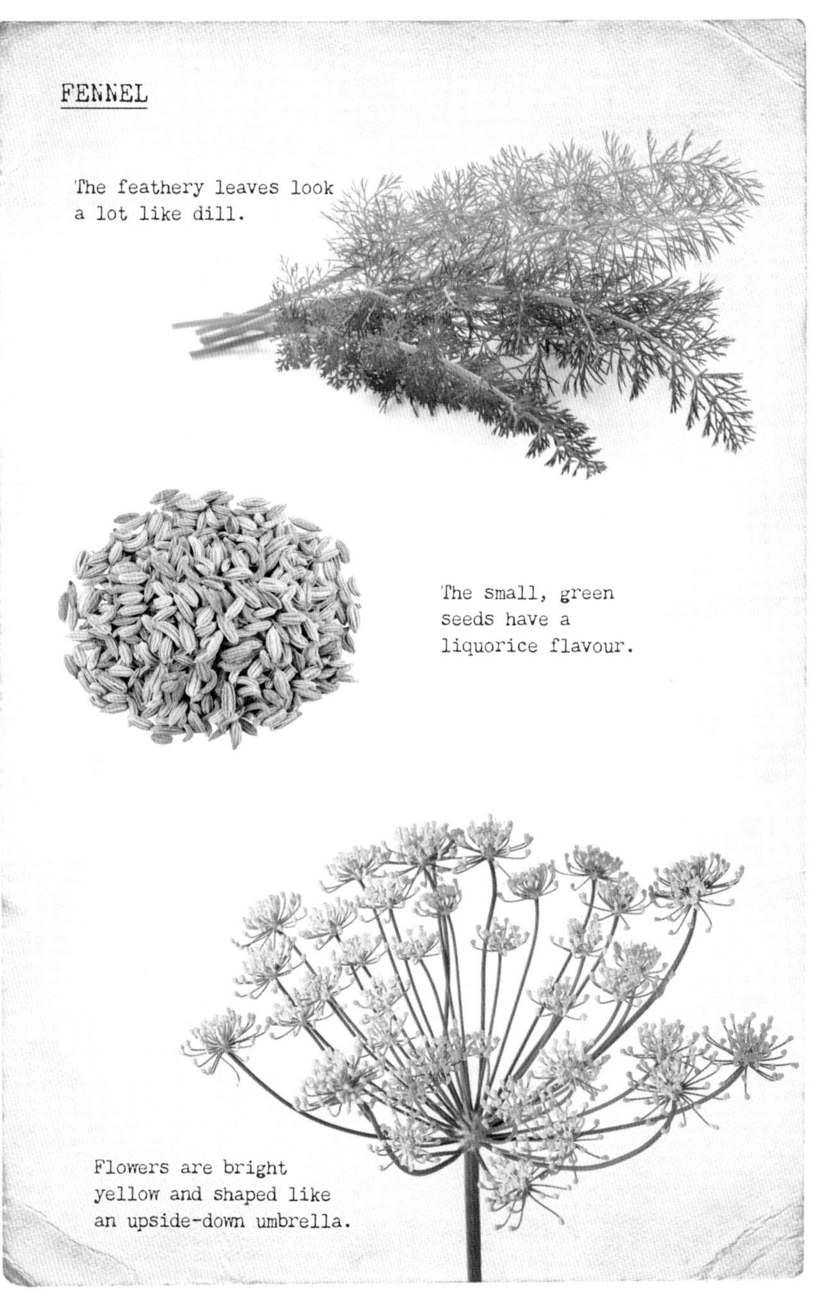
FENNEL
The feathery leaves look
a lot like dill.
The small, green
seeds have a
liquorice flavour.
Flowers are bright
yellow and shaped like
an upside-down umbrella.

Lastly, turn to page 162 to double-check you are not picking hemlock. This may sound terrifying, and it's unlikely, but it is good practice to keep those checks and balances in place when foraging, especially when it comes to this family of plants. If you are still not sure, wait a year and come back to the same place. As I'll keep saying, foraging is a rewarding hobby for a lifetime, so take your time to check carefully.

Wild fennel doesn't form a substantial bulb, and it's illegal to dig it up. Pick the leaves sparingly so they will continue to grow. I sometimes add a few leaves to a wild salad. Also, the leaves or the seeds are great when making cordials or gin. This is because the liquorice taste can add a sort of sweetness, enhancing floral flavours, meaning you can reduce the sugar in a mixer or in the cordial itself.

I love to pair the seeds with white fish when making fish *en papillote*, which means baked fish in greaseproof paper. I simply sprinkle a few seeds on top of the fish, seal it in greaseproof paper and then bake on a moderate heat for 20–30 minutes depending on the size of the fish and the type of oven.

You can also use fennel seeds to lift the flavour of a dish or vegetable. Try with beetroots, tomatoes and vegan nut 'cheeses'. Or, my absolute favourite, roasted carrots. They can also be used to flavour desserts, pairing well with ginger and citrus fruits.

Garlic mustard

Alliaria petiolata

Two of the common names for garlic mustard give you a clue to its habitat: namely, jack-by-the-hedge or hedge garlic. The patches I pick from are all next to, or under, local hedgerows. You can also find it growing across the understorey in forests.

As garlic mustard is a biennial, it takes two years to complete its growth cycle. Or, in other words, it might not always look the same. The initial growth is a basal (close to the ground) rosette (cluster of leaves). So initially look for a circle of leaves growing close to the ground.

At this early stage, the kidney-shaped leaves are around 4–8 centimetres (1½–3¼ inches) long and are similar in width or slightly wider. You'll start to spot these in the early spring, just as the weather is starting to warm up: around the time when the leaves are getting bigger, the first hawthorn leaves are starting to grow and the bird numbers are increasing. This is another plant you can positively identify by smell; crush up the leaves and give them a sniff, they should be quite garlicky.

AT A GLANCE

Where they grow

Hedgerows and woodland.

Brief description

Smells of garlic.

Lookalikes

Older plants can resemble nettles.

Dangers

All leaves contain water-soluble cyanide; be cautious and blanch or boil before consumption.

Conservation notes

From May to June look out for the orange eggs of the orange-tip butterfly; otherwise common enough to pick in abundance.

When to harvest

Spring–summer.

Use in

Leaf stems as a vegetable; pesto; very sparingly in *horta vrasta* (Greek boiled leafy greens) and salads.

Fun fact

In Holland the plant is known as *look-zonder-look*, which means 'see without looking' as it is so common.

GARLIC MUSTARD

The leaves look
a bit like broad
stinging nettles.

Young leaves smell
like garlic when
rubbed.

The white flowers
have four petals and
grow in clusters.

As the season progresses, the plants start to grow, and can reach up to almost 1 metre (3¼ feet) in height, although often they tend to be smaller. They have long stalks or 'petioles'. The leaves also change shape: they keep their blunt serrated edges but begin to elongate. They can start to resemble the shape of a stinging nettle leaf, in the sense that they become triangular. You might also notice the small flowers appearing; these are white with four petals in a cross shape. The emerging seeds look like long spikes.

I like to eat the leaves at all stages. However, I might be alone in this. The leaf becomes rather more pungent as the season progresses and not everyone enjoys that flavour. Most prefer it in the first stages of growth. On late spring walks, you might find both stages of growth and so you can compare and contrast. Some people simply dislike the taste of the leaves altogether, although this can be overcome by smothering them in balsamic (or pine needle) vinegar.

A quick harvesting lesson: many plants offer different flavours that can vary according to the season, age and location of the plant. Just because you don't like one plant, doesn't mean to say you won't like them all. In the case of garlic mustard, neither the leaf stem nor the stem of the plant have quite the same kick or flavour as the leaf. New growth can be succulent and delicious. Try the stalks steamed or fried in a little bit of butter or cold pressed rapeseed oil.

Fermented garlic mustard

This tasty recipe comes from Szymon Szyszczakiewicz of Foragerium.

Being from the cabbage family, garlic mustard has a flavour profile similar to some of its cousins - think horseradish, wasabi, mustard, white cabbage, mizuna or rocket. The chemical compounds responsible for the typical cabbage smell or fiery mustard flavours are called volatile sulphur compounds. 'Volatile' is a key word here; once fermented, plants in the cabbage family lose their characteristic taste profile as the sulphur compounds evaporate and the flavours become milder and softer. Yet often they remain crunchy, juicy, sour and are tastier than when eaten fresh. In Georgia, Armenia, Azerbaijan and the surrounding areas, garlic mustard is fermented. Always look for fresh growth and don't pick old and stringy plants. They should snap off readily, like fresh asparagus tips. Young and tender plants can be harvested just above the root.

Ingredients

1kg/2lb 4oz fresh garlic mustard
15-25g/½-1oz good quality salt

Method

Wash the garlic mustard in cold water. Drain well. Chop into 5cm (2in) pieces.

In a large bowl, mix together the garlic mustard and salt. Massage gently and leave to stand for 20 mins.

Start layering your salty mixture into the jar. Take your time and take care to push down each layer to expel as much air as possible. All plant matter should be submerged, and a 3-5cm space should be left at the top to allow for expansion.

Cover with a lid and ferment for 14 days at 15-18°C.

After 2 weeks it will be ready. You can either keep in the fridge and consume within a month, or pack tightly into smaller jars and keep in the fridge for up to 2 years.

Giant puffball

Calvatia gigantea

This is the only mushroom you'll find in this book, as I believe it is one of the tastiest and easiest to spot. It is also a delight to find – the sight of one makes me giggle with joy. This is partly due to their size; they are pretty much just a great big hunk of food, and just one large specimen can provide a good meal for all the family.

Giant puffballs are large and white and can look rather alien in an otherwise green landscape – this makes them easy to spot. It also means that anything white and alien-looking can be easily mistaken for one by the over-eager forager. One August, I ran into a field inhabited by a bull to retrieve a good-sized mushroom. Only it wasn't: it was half a football, and I narrowly escaped a mauling from the now-angry beast!

Giant puffballs are sufficiently common that the average grassland rambler, with their eyes peeled, can expect to find at least one when out and about during the summer months.

You may find a single puffball, although they often grow in large rings. Apparently,

AT A GLANCE

Where they grow

Mainly grassland, especially with cattle; also, beneath hedges, grass verges/next to paths, hiding among nettles.

Brief description

Large, round/ovoid and white (30cm/12in or more in diameter).

Lookalikes

The mosaic puffball – also edible. The mosaic puffball has warts on its skin.

Dangers

Lycoperdonosis (see main text). The emerging 'egg' of the death cap mushroom is much smaller than a giant puffball and should be avoided at all costs.

Harvest notes

Found July–September; when ripe, it is firm and pure white throughout.

Use in

See 'How to cook' (page 56).

Fun fact

Its Latin name literally means 'giant bald skull'.

GIANT PUFFBALL

Avoid small puffballs as these could be the 'eggs' of poisonous mushrooms.

Sliced puffballs look like mozzarella cheese.

They are big and can grow to the size of a beach ball.

these rings can be home to as many as 50 mushrooms, but I've never seen quite that many at once. Expect to find smaller groups of just a few or up to about 20. When you do find one, crouch down to its level and look in every direction. This is a foragers 'trick' for finding all the mushrooms in a ring.

The other distinguishing feature is their size; they can grow to the size of a beach ball. So, if you find something big, white and round in a field that isn't a football or a carrier bag, then you're onto a winner. When you cut open a perfect giant puffball, you'll find the inside is fleshy, solid and bright white, rather like a huge, firm mozzarella cheese.

If you find one that is golf ball-sized or smaller, leave it well alone. It could be the emerging 'egg' of any of the mushrooms in the genus *Amanita*. These include the death cap mushroom (*Amanita phalloides*), and are responsible for 95 per cent of all mushroom fatalities.

These 'eggs' are small, averaging less than 6 centimetres (2½ inches) in diameter. In comparison, the average size of a giant puffball is about 30 centimetres (12 inches) in diameter. Also, when you cut open a mushroom 'egg', you'll find the small white mushroom waiting to emerge.

Once puffballs start to get old, they will turn yellow and then darken to a toasted marshmallow brown. They are not edible at this stage. You can test their edibility by poking with a stick. If it is squidgy, leave it alone as it's starting to spore.

The spores on mature specimens can cause lycoperdonosis, a particularly nasty lung disease. Medical literature suggests that this only happens after inhaling a large number of spores, which only tends to happen if you are a dog, or you do this intentionally. So if you do have an inquisitive dog (or child), perhaps keep them close as a precaution.

There haven't been any confirmed cased of lycoperdonosis in the UK since the 1960s, and only two in America in the last 40 years. It can be completely avoided by staying away from mature specimens and only picking bright white young puff balls. However, if you do find that you are suffering from fever, chills, a productive cough or are feeling generally unwell, do seek medical advice.

How to cook

Some people prepare giant puffballs by peeling off the hard outer layer, especially on specimens that have been in the fridge for a while, or have been caked in mud, dirt and general outdoor detritus. It's not inedible, but can be tough. Sometimes a small insect can get inside a puffball and cause some browning. These blemishes are best cut out before washing and eating.

I tend to cook them very simply, frying slices in butter, retaining as much of the original 'clean'-tasting mushroom as possible.

There are many recipes online for giant puffball pizza bases. To make these, brush slices with oil and lightly grill before adding your favourite toppings. Then bake in a hot oven for 10–15 minutes, just as you would a regular pizza. This mushroom sucks in flavours and so can be fried in teriyaki sauce, miso, stout or any other strong flavour you enjoy.

Lastly, it can be stuffed and makes a great centrepiece for any dinner party. Simply slice off a 'lid' and hollow out the inside leaving at least a 3-centimetre (1¼-inch) wall of mushroom.

Fry the flesh up in a mix that can include bacon, aubergine, ham, onion, garlic, peppers, tomatoes or any vegetables of your choosing. You can bulk it out with a little couscous, oatmeal, pearl barley or rice.

Place the hollowed-out puffball on a baking dish, put the mixture back inside and replace the lid. The whole thing can then be baked for around 1–2 hours (depending on its size) at 180°C/160°C fan/350°F/gas 4.

GORSE

Pick the flowers between
January and June.

The spikes can be
vicious.

Gorse

Ulex europaeus

Gorse is a plant that I love and hate. I love the scent wafting in the breeze and drinking gorse flower wine or mead, which could have been snatched from the banqueting hall of the gods. Used in cocktails and sorbets, and perhaps mixed with a little pineapple weed, you may well feel a sense of the tropical. So, what is there to hate?

Picking – that's what. Gorse is a prickly bush that is very commonly found across Britain. I've been picking these flowers for about 20 years, and I still haven't quite got the knack of how to do it without hurting myself. Obviously, gloves would be a good idea, but I never seem to have them with me when I come across a big patch.

I've found gorse next to rivers, on roadsides and roundabouts, in heathland, woodland, near the sea and in undisturbed grassland. You'll often see shocks of yellow when travelling along a motorway.

It's said that the flowers can be found 'whenever kissing is in season', which one would hope means all year round. In practice, this is only partly true, as gorse does tend to flower sporadically. However,

AT A GLANCE

Where they grow

Verges; ungrazed land; wild places.

Brief description

Spiky bush; bright yellow flowers.

Lookalikes

Broom (*Cytisus*) is harmful if eaten and looks similar but crucially lacks the spines of gorse.

Dangers

The spikes!

Conservation notes

Try not to disturb nesting birds.

When to harvest

Flowers January–June.

Use in

Cocktails; desserts.

Fun fact

It's said that gorse flowers 'whenever kissing is in season' – i.e. most of the year!

the best plan is to don a pair of gloves, and head out any time between New Year's Day and Midsummer Day in late June.

What you are looking for is a shrub, often with many stems. Think bush rather than tree. Common gorse can grow to up to 2.5 metres (8 feet) in height, but I've only really found this to be the case in very wild and remote places and along hedgerows. About shoulder height is often the norm in urban places.

The simplest way to extract the flavour from the flowers is to infuse them for 10 minutes in water that is just off the boil, as you would when making a herbal tea. Then filter and use the liquid in place of any liquid in a recipe. The higher the concentration of flowers you use, the greater the flavour. You can also infuse the flowers for up to three days in alcohol; by far the greatest mead I've ever had was made with gorse flowers.

Ground ivy

ale-hoof

Glechoma hederacea

Ground ivy is also known as 'ale-hoof', because it was used in brewing to give the brew a tannic, bitter flavour. It was also employed as a fining agent, clarifying the beer by stabilising the tiny protein particles that remain in suspension and otherwise cause it to look murky.

I once found myself foraging around a beautiful and abundant wild area along the canal near the Carlsberg brewery in Northampton. It seemed very fitting that there were great swathes of ale-hoof growing everywhere and I imagined brewers of the past planting the herb for use in their ales. However, my romantic view of the brewery was soon shattered when I discovered it was founded in 1973.

Ground ivy can grow up to 1 metre (3¼ feet) in height. However, I often find it at much lower levels, especially in the first half of the year. Given the right conditions, it will spread out and is often found growing at the base of trees. Its leaves are kidney-shaped (described by some as heart-shaped) and they are framed with rounded teeth.

AT A GLANCE

Where they grow

Woodland edges; damp places.

Brief description

Dead-nettle-like plant, with a square stem and rounded leaves.

Lookalikes

Dead-nettles; henbit.

Dangers

Avoid when pregnant and breastfeeding.

Conservation notes

Common and widespread, but only pick what you need as this plant is important for pollinating insects.

When to harvest

Spring–autumn.

Use in

Dishes that require thyme; home-brewed beer; simply as a tea; sparingly in a salad.

Fun fact

Ground ivy was famed in the nineteenth century as a remedy for gout and rheumatism.

The leaves grow opposite one another, and they are individually attached to the square stem of the plant. The flowers are small, trumpet-like and pale blue to violet, appearing from late spring to summer in groups of two to four tubular flowers with 'lips' that have three lobes on the bottom lip and two on top.

You can also identify ground ivy by the smell, which is unique. Some describe it as a mixture of blackcurrant cordial and tomcat urine. I think it's rather more earthy than that, with a hint of the woodland. Either way, don't let the smell put you off the taste, which has hints of mint, pine, thyme and pepper.

Ground ivy and mint sauce

I find that a simple mint sauce is given a rounder and earthier flavour with the addition of ground ivy and pairs wonderfully with roast lamb, venison or rich vegan sausages.

Ingredients

15g/½oz fresh ground ivy leaves
15g/½oz fresh mint leaves
15g/½oz sugar
50ml/2fl oz boiling water
30ml/2 tablespoons white wine vinegar

Method

Finely cut the leaves, place in a bowl and pound slightly with a blunt wooden object of your choice.

Pour the sugar into a tea cup, add the boiling water and stir until dissolved. Next, pour the sugar mixture over the leaves. Allow to cool a little and then add the vinegar.

Leave to stand for 30 mins until the flavours are fully combined. The sauce will keep for up to a year.

GROUND IVY

The purple, trumpet-like flowers can be seen from March-June.

The kidney shaped leaves have rounded edges.

Hazelnut

Corylus avellana

Hazelnuts are one of the most frustrating things to forage. More often than not you'll be fighting the squirrels or the jays for them. Occasionally, you'll find a precious few on the ground, only to find they are empty, having been eaten by grubs. Still, in the few areas that are empty of grey squirrels, you may be lucky enough to find some.

Ancient Britons enjoyed hazel as a major carbohydrate source. So, if you get a chance, plant some. It might be welcomed by future generations. Some even speculate that the first form of currency in Britain and across Europe might have been the hazelnut.

If left unpruned, hazel can grow up to 6 metres (20 feet) in height. The nuts are small and brown, and grow in a kind of green sleeve. You may already know what they look like, but if not this is another plant that you can check in a shop. Many good greengrocers will sell hazelnuts from around September onwards. These are exactly the same nuts you will be harvesting.

The coarse leaves on the tree are rounded and serrated with a point at the end. The

AT A GLANCE

Where they grow

Hedgerows; native planting in parks; woodlands; cliffs.

Brief description

Understorey tree bearing little brown nuts in autumn.

Lookalikes

Leaves can be mistaken for lime. Nuts could be mistaken for horse chestnuts, at a push, but conkers are much larger and come in a spiked shell.

Dangers

Angry squirrels and nut allergies.

When to harvest

September–October.

Use in

Roasted and infused in whisky; in cakes; raw; in a wild pesto.

Fun fact

Turkey is the world's largest hazelnut producer with around 70 per cent of international supply originating there.

HAZELNUT
Ripe hazelnuts; get them before the squirrels do.
The male catkins consist of 240 individual flowers.
Hazelnuts grow in small green sleeves and darken as they ripen.

catkins are often one of the only things growing in the winter months and they hang down like joyful yellow caterpillars. If you make a mental note of where you see these in the winter, you can return the following autumn.

Crack the nuts and eat them raw, or roast to bring out their flavour. Place a single layer of shelled nuts on a baking tray and roast at 180°C/160°C fan/350°F/gas 4 for about 10–15 minutes, or toast in a frying pan if you are short on time. In both cases, they are done when the delicious smell of roasted nuts fills the kitchen and they have gone a darker brown. If they are starting to turn black they are overdone.

Use roasted and crushed in pasta dishes, stuffings, nut roasts; in biscotti to replace pistachios; and as an ingredient in native pesto. They pair really well with chocolate and also make a great cocktail – the hazelnut Manhattan.

Hazelnut Manhattan

A good stiff drink, ideal for sipping in front of a fire. To make hazelnut bourbon, place 400g (14oz) of roasted and chopped hazelnuts and 500ml (18fl oz) Bourbon in a jar. Allow to infuse for 3 days and then filter and decant. It will keep for around a year but deteriorates a little after 6 months.

Ingredients

2 parts hazelnut bourbon
1 part Italian sweet vermouth
4 dashes of Angostura bitters

Method

Combine, pour over ice and stir.

Horseradish

Armoracia rusticana

Old English cookbooks will often refer to anything that is strong, large or coarse as being 'horse'. You may have heard of horse mushrooms or horse mint, for example. *Horse*radish, then, is a large, coarse and strong radish.

This is not a bad description, as wild horseradish fits all of those descriptors in spades – as you'll find when you first dig some up and prepare it. First, you'll be struck by just how far down this root can travel, then by the coarseness of the root itself as you wash and peel it. Lastly, the pungent aroma released when grating will sort out any sinus problems for anyone in the immediate vicinity.

Horseradish is native to the UK. Harvest with the landowner's permission, but they may be glad of some help removing a patch as it can really take hold. Getting permission is often fairly straightforward: just be polite, respectful and as charming as you can. Offer to share the final dish with them.

Even when you do manage to get most of the root out, there always seems to be a small finger left in the ground, which will be

AT A GLANCE

Where they grow

Once-cultivated land.

Brief description

Large, thick-leaved plant.

Lookalikes

Dock; many other plants if digging up the root when leaves have died down.

Dangers

Mistaking the root for a poisonous plant like Monk's-hood. To avoid this, only dig up until late October.

Conservation notes

Look out for butterfly eggs before picking the leaves, including the single eggs of the small white butterfly.

When to harvest

Leaves in summer; roots in autumn.

Use in

As a condiment; in vodka.

Fun fact

In Greek mythology, the Oracle of Delphi told Apollo that horseradish was worth its weight in gold.

HORSERADISH
Clusters of white flowers appear May-July.
Mature leaves are large, thick and glossy.
The knobbly roots have a pungent, sinus-clearing smell when grated.

enough for the whole plant to grow right back up again. If you can remember where you found your precious root, you won't need to search for any again in subsequent years.

I've found horseradish growing on the edges of fields, on wild lands and close to disused railway lines. It seems most common around cities and is not so common in open countryside. Look for it close to allotments and in abandoned Victorian gardens.

This is another plant where you can use shops to help with identification. Find a deli or greengrocer that stocks fresh horseradish root. Peel a little off and smell it; make sure to remember that smell when you dig up wild horseradish.

The most distinguishing feature is the size of the leaves. By midsummer, these can grow up to 1 metre (3¼ feet) long, from the tip of the leaf to the stem. It's easy to confuse the leaves with dock, however, as those of horseradish are thick, glossy and vivid green with the texture of cabbage leaves (to which they are related). The leaves are also bluntly serrated. To be 100 per cent sure, crumple a leaf in your hand and give it a good sniff. Does it remind you of the smell of your shop-bought horseradish root?

I'd suggest only digging up the plant when the leaves are growing. The roots will be good to eat right up until the spring, but the leaves will die down. Get to know the plant and the area it grows in near you.

Horseradish shouldn't just live on the side of a dinner plate next to a Sunday pub lunch of roast beef. You could try using it in drinks (see overleaf).

Horseradish bloody Mary

This delicious recipe came to me via a Russian friend, Sasha Kotcho-Williams.

Ingredients

1 large, fresh horseradish root
1 litre/1¾ pints of good vodka
25ml/5 teaspoons of honey (or dandelion honey if vegan)

Method

Peel the horseradish root and then slice it carefully with a very sharp knife into long, thin slivers of about 10cm - you should end up with 12-15 of them. Place them in a thoroughly cleaned bottle. Pour a little vodka into a small glass and stir in the honey until it dissolves, then pour this over the horseradish slivers. Pour the rest of the vodka into the bottle up to the neck, covering the horseradish.

Leave in a dark place to infuse for 3-4 days, after which pour it through a colander or sieve, discarding the horseradish, and return to a clean bottle. Use within 3-4 months.

For the bloody Mary

60ml/4 tablespoons horseradish vodka
Juice of half a lemon
6-8 dashes of Worcestershire sauce (or vegan alternative*)
3 dashes of Tabasco sauce
150ml/5 fl oz tomato juice
Salt and freshly ground black pepper

* You could try mixing 2 parts ketchup, 2 parts pine needle vinegar with 1 part soy sauce as an alternative to Worcestershire sauce.

Method

Fill a tall glass with ice. Pour in the vodka with the lemon juice and add all the other ingredients apart from the salt and pepper. Stir and season to taste.

Rosehip and horseradish sauce

The first time I discovered that horseradish and rosehips pair really well together was when I saw a recipe combining them both by fellow forager and friend Liz Knight. So, naturally I tried fermenting them together.

Many of the foods we now enjoy pickled, such as eggs and onions, were originally fermented. I'd highly recommend trying out fermenting if you have the time, it can make a refreshing alternative to pickling.

This recipe might not seem like a bed of roses to prepare, but I'm sure you will be really pleased with the results. It is one of those recipes that never fails to wow an audience.

Ingredients

250g/9oz grated horseradish
60g/2¼oz de-seeded rosehips
60ml/4 tablespoons filtered or unchlorinated water*
15ml/1 tablespoon water from a previous ferment (if available)
5g/1 teaspoon sea salt
5ml/1 teaspoon apple cider vinegar
5ml/1 teaspoon honey
5g/1 teaspoon black mustard seeds or wild garlic seeds (optional)

* Leave tap water uncovered overnight and the chlorine will evaporate - a method known as off-gassing.

Method

Grate the horseradish root and prepare the rosehips. This is a great job if you have a cold or sinus trouble, but it's not so good in a confined space or if you are sensitive to smells. Depending on your tolerance level, you may wish to wear goggles as it can make the eyes stream. You can also wear something to protect your nostrils, such as a face mask.

Layer the inside of your jar with one layer of grated horseradish root then cover with rosehips. Repeat the process until you get to the top of the jar. You can add more rosehips if you wish for a lighter sauce.

Boil a small amount of the water, stir in the salt until fully dissolved, and then top up with the rest of the cold water.

Pour the resulting brine into the jar and weigh it down. Cover with a small piece of material or tea towel to keep out any airborne pests. Add the water from your previous ferment if available.

Leave for 3-5 days, ensuring that it begins to bubble within this time. Once it has fermented, gently pour out most of the water. You'll need to retain a little to help the food processor do its job - you can use the excess liquid for another fermentation or to start another batch of sauce.

Scoop out the contents of the jar and place them into the blender with a small amount of the water and blend into a rough paste. Stir in the vinegar and honey. I also like to stir in a teaspoon of black mustard seeds to give a little crunch.

Serve with lamb, game and other rich meats.

Japanese knotweed

Reynoutria japonica (syn. *Fallopia japonica*)

Japanese knotweed is quite a remarkable plant, but you don't want it near your property. It can grow up to 3 metres (10 feet) tall at a rate of 3 centimetres (7½ inches) every day and can survive temperatures of -35°C (-31°F). To ensure that you have eliminated it, you have to dig down up to 3 metres (10 feet) to get out every last bit of the root, incinerating the soil. Even then it has been known to return. It can grow through tarmac and even up through foundations. All this means mortgage companies will refuse to lend on properties where it is growing.

However, as a forager I love it, as it tastes like a better version of rhubarb. In April, just as everything else is coming alive, you'll see the new shoots poking out of the ground or the road. When searching for this plant, it's often easier to find an existing patch.

The previous year's growth will look a bit like bamboo poles sticking out of the ground. After April, it will be getting

AT A GLANCE

Where they grow

Riversides; building sites; railway embankments; cemeteries; waste dumps.

Brief description

Huge plant, up to 3m/10ft; highly invasive.

Lookalikes

Triffids.

Dangers

Sprayed plants. If you are unsure if a plant has been sprayed, ask the landowner or avoid and look elsewhere.

Conservation notes

Pick to your heart's content but be careful not to spread it – this is illegal even if done accidentally; always burn any leftovers.

When to harvest

April.

Use in

Any rhubarb recipe.

Fun fact

An orange dye can be obtained from the root of Japanese knotweed, and it has been successfully used in screen printing.

JAPANESE KNOTWEED
The heart-shaped leaves grow on zig-zagging stems that resemble bamboo.
Clusters of creamy-white flowers appear in August and September.
Pick the young shoots when they are the size of asparagus.

pretty big and the heart-shaped leaves will have unfurled. The plant grows in nodes or sections, almost as if it is made from interlocking pieces.

Often there are skinny shoots and fatter shoots – it's the fatter ones you are after, and only the first 20 centimetres (8 inches) or so of growth. These are green with red speckles and have a kind of skirt separating each node. At the top, the emerging leaves will cluster in a crown shape. Later in the season you can harvest the longer shoots, but they need to be peeled.

It is worth noting that Japanese knotweed can grow from the tiniest remains of a plant. So, don't compost your leftovers or peelings – burn them. Allowing this plant to spread is illegal.

The plant can be eaten both sweet and savoury just like rhubarb. It is not as tart as rhubarb, but it still works well with sweeter flavours to temper it.

Nutty knotweed nibbles

There is a gooey texture and a richness to these knotweed nibbles that will have you coming back for more. The first time I ever baked them I sat and ate the whole batch - think rocky road or chocolate fondant, but with buttery nuts and a tang of rhubarb instead of chocolate.

Ingredients

100g/3½oz butter
100g/3½oz chopped hazelnuts
100g/3½oz unrefined golden sugar
5g/1 teaspoon mixed spice
175g/6oz light brown muscovado sugar
1 egg
300g/10½oz Japanese knotweed
225g/8oz plain flour
5g/1 teaspoon baking soda
280ml/9½fl oz sour cream

Method

Preheat oven to 180°C/160°C fan/350°F/gas 4.

Put ½ oz/15g of the butter in a dish, and place it in the oven for 2 mins until melted. Remove, stir in the hazelnuts, golden sugar and mixed spice. Set aside.

Cream the rest of the butter, the muscovado sugar and egg until fully blended. Cut the knotweed into small penny-sized rounds; any larger pieces should be cut in half. Stir in all the rest of the ingredients apart from the nut mixture.

Place in a large round cake tin and spread the mixture to a depth of about 3cm/1 inch. Sprinkle over the nut mix and bake for 40 mins or until fully cooked. Push a skewer into the centre of the cake and take it out again; if it comes out clean it is done.

Allow to cool, then cut into nibble-sized pieces.

Lemon balm

Melissa officinalis

Strictly speaking, this isn't a wild plant but more of an escapee. Lemon balm readily evades its garden confines and utilises the tiniest pockets of soil – hence its inclusion here. I've spotted it growing in between paving slabs, on narrow grass verges, next to gravestones, on roadsides and in a neighbour's flower bed. I have a sneaking suspicion that the latter has seeded from a single original plant – mine!

The plant itself is very similar to a dead-nettle or stinging nettle, but with small, white or pale purple, flute-like flowers that bloom in the summer sun. Depending on soil and sunlight conditions, its leaves can vary from a lemon green to a darker bottle green. The plant can grow up to 1 metre (3¼ feet), at which point it will have seeded and you can sometimes hear the seed pods rattling in the wind.

Lemon balm is another plant that can be identified by smell. Pick a leaf and crush it in your hand. It will give off a lemony scent; not the note of citrus you get from the zest of a lemon, but rather the deeper lemon scent of the pulp.

AT A GLANCE

Where they grow

Often as an escapee, close to settlements.

Brief description

Nettle-like plant.

Lookalikes

Stinging nettles and dead-nettles.

Dangers

Mistaking for a stinging nettle and getting stung!

Conservation notes

Spreads easily and widely cultivated. Some landowners might welcome picking. Still, leave a bit of root in the ground for next year's crop.

When to harvest

Late spring before flowering.

Use in

Herbal tea and dishes where you'd normally use lemon.

Fun fact

Country folk say of lemon balm that 'Its virtue is only released when crushed.'

LEMON BALM

The plant produces creamy-white or pale purple flowers in summer.

The lemon-scented leaves look like 'soft' stinging nettles.

I use this herb predominately as a middle-of-the-night tea when I wake up and can't get back to sleep again. I use around two teaspoons of dried herb. The late Stephen Buhner, herbalist extraordinaire, also promoted its use in treating cold sores as its antiviral properties can boost the immune system. In this case, it must be used fresh, as drying the leaves reduces the scent and therefore the active medicinal ingredients.

But this plant is more than just a medicinal herb. It can add a lovely subtle, fresh lemon flavour when chopped up into a salad, or gives bit of a lift when added to white sauce for fish. I like to combine it with a little bit of fennel, while others suggest tarragon. You can also use it in desserts in place of lemon. In fact, just think of instances where you might add a little bit of lemon juice, and add a few finely chopped lemon balm leaves instead.

LIME
The bark is pale grey-brown with irregular ridges.
The young leaves can be picked for salads.
Flowers appear in June and July; note the papery green bract on the flower stem.

Lime

Tilia spp.

It's easy to forget that many different parts of tree can be eaten – the lime is one of these. They flank many Victorian parks, so shouldn't be hard to find.

Lime can be tapped for sap and the mature fruits can be eaten. However, it's the blossom and the leaves that are by far the easiest to harvest.

The younger leaves are good to eat and these start to appear in late spring; they can continue to grow and flourish on sucker growth. The blossoms appear around midsummer in the south of the UK, and towards the end of the summer or even into very early autumn in the far northern islands of Scotland.

When I'm out foraging in spring and summer, I often pass by two particular trees, plucking off a few leaves and munching on them as I go. Both trees are surrounded by many new shoots (known as suckers), and when foraging with a focus I can easily pick enough leaves for a salad. I aim for the smallest, shiniest leaves as they are the tastiest. However, some people hate the texture of lime leaves.

AT A GLANCE

Where they grow

Parks; gardens; woodlands.

Brief description

Tall trees with heart-shaped leaves.

Lookalikes

Hazelnut and other trees with similar leaves; look for other distinguishing features.

Dangers

Allergies.

When to harvest

Leaves in May–June; blossom in midsummer; fruit late summer.

Use in

Leaves in salads; blossom as a herbal tea; fruits as chocolate substitute.

Fun fact

The blossom from one single lime tree can yield enough nectar to make 2.5kg/5½lb of honey.

For them, the lime can still delight with its midsummer blossom. Foragers, bees and aphids alike will buzz around them in search of this wild food superstar. It can be used simply to make a delicious tea. All you need are a few clusters of the flowers steeped in hot water for 5 minutes or so. Many swear that it helps their digestion and will drink it after meals. Herbalists also tout its anti-anxiety properties.

I warn you though, if you do get a taste for lime blossom tea, there is a very small picking window. They quickly turn into the small fruits that don't make good tea. As already mentioned, the harvest time also varies depending on where you are in the UK.

I dry the blossoms over a week to ten days by simply placing them on newspaper in a well-ventilated room and turning them, which intensifies their flavour. Store them in an airtight container. They can then be relied upon right up until midsummer the following year.

As with all edible flowers, I like to add them to my gin creations with a few juniper berries. Fellow forager John Rensten likes to make a lime flower champagne, produced in a similar way to elderflower champagne (where the flowers are infused in a sugar solution and then fermented), but using lime blossoms instead.

Then there is the fruit, known as linden nuts. Believe it or not, you can use these 'nuts' to make a chocolate substitute.

Linden chocolate

This recipe comes courtesy of my Tennessean friend, Ashlyn Morgan. She attempted to replicate early descriptions of processing linden nuts into a paste resembling chocolate. These accounts date back to the eighteenth century. Historical recipes, often devoid of detail, require one to fill in the gaps. In this recipe, the added steps of roasting the linden nuts and including sugar are important for creating a simple spread that can reasonably be compared to the flavours of chocolate, toffee and black tea.

Ingredients

5g/1 teaspoon dried lime flowers
80g/2¾oz young, green linden nuts
100ml/3½fl oz grapeseed oil
60g/2¼oz icing sugar

Method

Preheat the oven to 190°C/170°C fan/375°F/gas 5.

Grind the dried lime flowers into a fine powder using a pestle and mortar or electric grinder. Set aside.

Evenly disperse the linden nuts on a baking sheet and roast for 25-30 mins or until brittle and rich brown in colour. Remove from the oven and let cool.

Grind the roasted linden nuts into a fine powder using a pestle and mortar or electric grinder. If necessary, use a sieve to remove any remaining large pieces or fibres.

In a bowl, combine the ground lime flowers, ground linden nuts, grapeseed oil and icing sugar. Mix until thoroughly combined.

Enjoy by the spoonful or spread on toast and biscuits as you would a chocolate hazelnut spread.

MAGNOLIA

Darker blossoms can be used dried as a substitute for ginger.

Make sure you get permission before picking magnolia blossom.

Magnolia

Magnolia spp.

When local forager Martin Bailey first introduced me to the blossoms of the magnolia tree I was astonished. It's a tree I've seen brightening up front gardens across suburban Britain every spring, and it is actually edible?

Martin plucked a single flower bud from a tree and told me to take just one small bite. Tentatively, I did so. It tasted of ginger and parma violets, along with a hint of nothing else I'd ever tasted before. This was a brand new experience, exactly the sort of taste exploration foraging should be about.

Magnolias can be trees that grow up to 30 metres (100 feet) in height or much smaller shrubs. The leaves are ovate (egg-shaped) with veins running up from the central vein – the midrib. They become far more distinctive when budding. Hairy little khaki-coloured buds will start to appear; these can grow up to 10 centimetres (4 inches) long in some species. As the spring temperatures rise, the blossoms will sprout. They range from showy, pink-red blossoms, to smaller, more sedate and sensible white ones.

AT A GLANCE

Where they grow

Parks and gardens.

Brief description

Trees or shrubs with ornate, showy blossoms.

Dangers

None reported – but extra research needed for less common species.

When to harvest

Early flowering varieties in spring; late flowering varieties in summer.

Use in

Pair with chocolate or anything that goes well with ginger.

Fun fact

The petals on a magnolia are not actually petals, they are tepals. They are not quite a sepal – protective outer petals – nor are they just petals, they are in between the two.

I like to ferment a few of the buds and use in place of ginger when making kimchi. I also cut up one or two 'petals' (actually tepals; see 'Fun fact' on the previous page) for the salad bowl, to add an extra-special something. Rob Gould, Cotswold forager, likes them with chocolate brownies and simply wraps a tepal around one before taking a bite.

Lastly, save a few buds for drying; this reduces any bitterness and helps preserve the unique flavour all year round. This can be used in place of ground ginger in many recipes (see opposite).

There are over 200 types of magnolia in the UK and their taste has been scrutinised by Kew Garden's forager, Kim Walker. She suggests fermenting or drying the darker-coloured buds, as they taste bitter and unpleasant when eaten raw. Whereas the lighter buds lose their flavour when dried and are much nicer eaten raw.

A word of caution: magnolias are often planted for their beauty. I strive for neighbourly equanimity and avoid picking from newly established trees. I'll also always ask the owner of the garden before picking; harvesting the very blossom for which the trees have been planted is not the best way to win friends and influence people. Pick only the inner blossoms, leaving the beauty for all to enjoy.

There is a general consensus in the foraging world that all magnolias are edible; however, there is not a huge amount of research to back this up. Each new variety should be treated with caution. That said, author Robin Harford of Eatweeds has compiled a list using ethnobotanical records and vouches for the following species: *Magnolia coco*, *M. grandiflora*, *M. denudata*, *M. obovata* (syn. *M. hypoleuca*), *M. kobus*, *M. mexicana*, *M. pterocarpa* and *M.* × *soulangeana*; and to that list I can personally add *M. stellata* and *M. liliiflora*.

Magnolia and knotweed snaps

If you have a friend who remains unconvinced about wild flavours then these simple snaps will win them over.

To dehydrate the magnolia and Japanese knotweed, place in the oven on the lowest setting and wedge the door open with something heat-resistant such as a wooden spoon. This will take around 3 hours, so keep checking. Or you can dehydrate at 40°C (104°F) if you have a dehydrator. You don't want either of the plants to dry out to the point that they crumble to the touch but neither do you want them to have any obvious moisture. Test by squeezing: they should be dry but with some sponginess. Once dried, both can be ground up in a coffee grinder or with a pestle and mortar.

Keep any left-over magnolia or knotweed powder in an air-tight container.

Ingredients

350g/12oz plain white flour
150g/5½oz granulated sugar
15g/3 teaspoons dried and powdered magnolia buds
5g/1 teaspoon dried and powdered Japanese knotweed
10g/2 teaspoons bicarbonate of soda
175ml/6fl oz golden syrup
150g/5½oz unsalted butter

Method

Mix together all the dry ingredients, ensuring the magnolia and knotweed are well-distributed.

Heat up the golden syrup, this makes it easier to work with. You can microwave for 1 min on ¾ power or heat gently in a pan. It doesn't have to be boiling hot, just warmed through.

At this point you can pre-heat the oven to 180°C/160°C fan/350°F/gas 4. Rub the butter into the dry ingredients until the mixture resembles breadcrumbs.

Pour in the golden syrup and mix until you have a brown dough. If it's too sticky add a little more flour.

Roll into balls that are somewhere between a walnut and a hazelnut in size. Each should weigh approx. 10g/0.3oz and they will need to be at least 7cm ($2\frac{3}{4}$in) in diameter.

Place on a greased or silicone-lined baking tray and bake for 10-15 mins or until they are golden brown and look like expensive ginger snaps.

Allow to cool slightly on the tray and then gently transfer to cool completely on a wire rack. Keep in an air-tight tin.

Mint

Mentha spp.

There are many types of mint out there, and they hybridise, meaning that new varieties pop up all the time. All mints have a square stem; twirl the plant between your fingers to check this, if it stutters when spun it's mint. Once you know the plant belongs to the mint family, the next step is to pick a leaf, crush it and smell it. Are you greeted with the pungent, refreshing smell of mint?

If you are still not sure then check the leaves – they look a bit like less angry nettles. They have the same serrated edges, only these are blunt and smooth; they look like they'll tickle rather than sting. If you are foraging in the summer, you will also find spikes of white or pink flowers.

To convince non-foraging friends of your new foraging prowess, serve them mojitos with your foraged mint. It's made with the juice of a lime, a teaspoon of sugar and a handful of mint leaves. Put all of these in a jug, pound the leaves with a muddler, the end of a rolling pin or a wooden spoon. Stir in some ice, then top up with two hefty shots of white rum. It's cocktail time!

AT A GLANCE

Where they grow

Abandoned gardens, close to cultivated areas; beside watercourses.

Brief description

Look for serrated leaf edges, a square stem and a smell of mint when the leaves are crushed.

Lookalikes

Nettles; dead-nettles.

Dangers

Liverflukes in stagnant water – pick only from flowing watercourses.

When to harvest

Spring–summer.

Use in

Cocktails; chutneys (see recipe overleaf); mint sauce.

Fun fact

The Ebers Papyrus, an Egyptian medical text dating back to 1550 BCE, cites mint as a remedy for flatulence.

Mint chutney

This is a great accompaniment to some of the hotter curries, and considering some of its ancient uses, your family may be particularly grateful (see Fun fact, page 89).

Ingredients

20g/¾oz/a small handful of mint leaves
10g/2 teaspoons golden caster sugar
250g/9oz natural yogurt
Juice of half a lime

Method

Place all the ingredients, bar the lime juice, into a blender and mix together until it is smooth and green. Chill in the fridge, and then when you are ready to serve, stir in the lime juice.

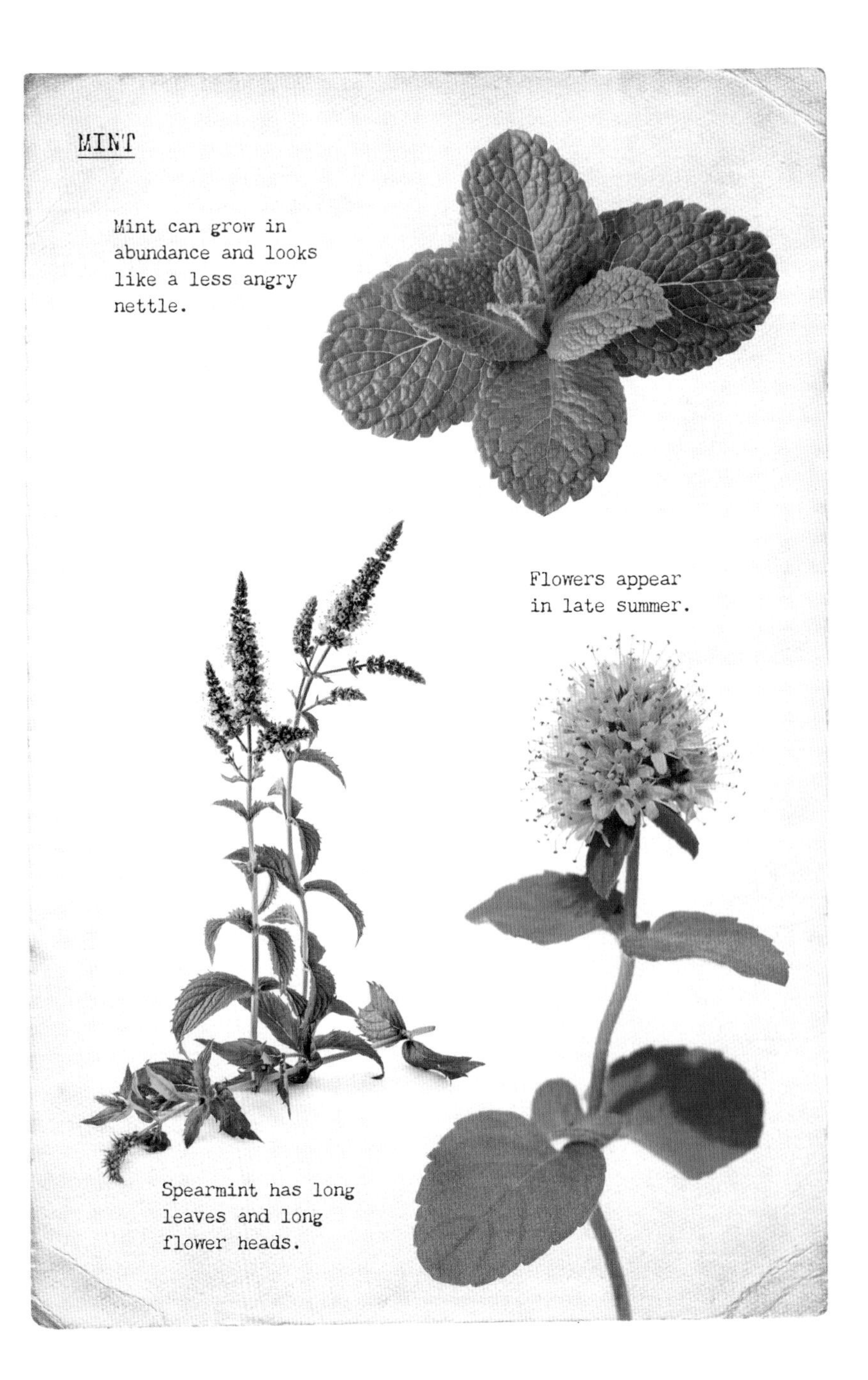

MINT

Mint can grow in abundance and looks like a less angry nettle.

Flowers appear in late summer.

Spearmint has long leaves and long flower heads.

MUGWORT
The green leaves are lobed and pointed.
The leaves have a lighter underside.
The flower buds are little round egg shapes.
Clusters of small red/brown flowers appear from early summer to autumn.

Mugwort

Artemisia vulgaris

I've heard mugwort being referred to as the traveller's friend. Perhaps this is because you'll often see it growing next to roadsides, pathways, canals, railway tracks and river banks. In fact, if you ever have the misfortune to be driving round the M25 in late summer, you'll see acres of the stuff growing spectacularly tall – not that I'd recommend foraging any there!

In wilder places, you'll be alerted to it by the remains of the previous year's growth, which can grow to around 1.75 metres (5¾ feet). Early leaves, found close to the ground, can be mistaken for poisonous Monk's-hood or ragwort (see pages 170 and 172 before picking). The stems are a little hairy and red-purple, with branches coming off them. Leaves are green and hairless above with pale grey hairy undersides. The edges of the leaves are pointed.

To the untrained eye the small flower heads hardly look like flowers at all. They are less than 0.5 centimetres (¼ inch) long. They start off red/brown in the summer and develop into tiny little grey/green egg shapes.

AT A GLANCE

Where they grow

River banks; byways; highways; disturbed ground.

Brief description

A unique smell; leaves that are silver/grey on the underside and green on top.

Lookalikes

Monk's-hood (Wolfsbane).

Dangers

Avoid if pregnant or breastfeeding and not advised if epileptic or on epilepsy medication.

When to harvest

While in flower in late summer.

Use in

Drinks; with rich meats.

Fun fact

Mugwort is known as a druidic herb in some circles. Mead made with mugwort was drunk in order to induce prophetic dreams.

Descriptions of the smell of mugwort vary from unpleasant, to somewhere between sage, cannabis or even rosemary. I love the smell: the crushed leaves are reminiscent of an alpine slope in spring or childhood memories of river banks.

Its distinct, aromatic, herby taste certainly lends itself to traditional European culinary uses, such as a stuffing for goose, pork and mutton. Used sparingly, it can also do wonders for cordials and vinegars, pairing especially well with elderberry. I love it in drinks. I put a leaf or two in a 250ml (8fl oz) jar of vodka, leave for a week and then strain. Add this to vermouths and gins, or perhaps to some strong dark beer, such as an imperial stout or porter.

In Japan, the leaves are soaked in water for a day to reduce bitterness and then used in various dishes. This is something to consider if you have the time and you struggle with the bitter end of the flavour spectrum.

Mulberry

Morus nigra

I first happened upon mulberries when I moved to Bristol. The fruit certainly looked edible, a bit like a large, squashy blackberry, but I wasn't going to take the risk. I pored over some identification guides to find out what they were. I returned a day later and had my fill.

I'd love it if you could experience the same joy, which is why I've included this somewhat rare tree here. These mouth-watering berries are tart and sweet at the same time. With a 90 per cent water content they squash very easily, making them almost impossible to transport and sell. This is why, despite being one of the world's great tastes, many people have never tried one.

There are at least two varieties of mulberry you might find growing in the UK. The tastiest and most common is the black mulberry (*Morus nigra*) and so that is what I'll focus on here.

Black mulberry trees can grow up to 12 metres (40 feet) tall. The rough leaves are 8–12 centimetres (3–5 inches) long, thick and dark green in colour. The leaves become coarser as the tree ages, and they come in

AT A GLANCE

Where they grow

Next to water; in parks and gardens.

Brief description

Straggly, low-growing tree with elongated black berries.

Lookalikes

Blackberries; raspberries.

Dangers

A book from the 1970s reports that the unripe fruits are hallucinogenic and cause severe nausea. I have found no further evidence, but I've never risked finding out, and suggest you do the same.

When to harvest

Late summer.

Fun fact

The song 'Here we go round the mulberry bush' is supposed to have originated at Wakefield Prison where one once grew in the exercise yard. The rhyme is said to have been invented by wives of inmates to keep their children occupied during prison visits.

MULBERRY
Male flowers form catkins.
The lobed or heart-shaped leaves are coarse.
Ripe fruits fall with the lightest pressure.
Late summer is the best time to harvest.

various shapes. Some are lobed and could be mistaken for a fig leaf; others are elegant and heart-shaped; and some look like they are struggling to decide on a shape and have two points or split before they have finished growing.

The fruits look a bit like a long raspberry or blackberry. Look closely and you'll see individual segmented fruits packed together to make up the berry we see. To forage, all you need to do is to tap the ripened berries and they will fall off. Don't pick wearing white clothes as the fruits can and will stain.

NASTURTIUM

The leaves are rounded with the stalk coming from a central point.

You can use the seeds to make capers.

Nasturtium flowers can vary in colour.

Nasturtiums regularly escape from gardens.

The edible flowers can add colour to salads.

Nasturtium

Tropaeolum spp.

Many years ago I led foraging courses at the Eden Project. I met many lovely people, including a very enthusiastic young boy. He was keen to sample everything, but I feared that the unprepared seeds of the nasturtium might be too much for less developed taste buds. After all, they are related to horseradish and wasabi, and do pack a punch. Instead, I suggested he offer them to his parents. This he duly did, and I can still see their trusting faces as they crunched down on these cannonballs of flavour, eyes streaming.

Nasturtiums are another garden escapee, and are known to regularly stray beyond the confines of suburban gardens. Come late summer, I see them trailing down over walls, jutting out of fences and generally spreading as far as they can go.

They are easy to spot as the flowers are often a shock of vivid oranges, reds and yellows. You might notice creams, salmon-pink, crimson and burgundy flowers too. Sometimes a single flower may sport more than one colour: yellow marbled with orange, for example.

AT A GLANCE

Where they grow

Escapees from gardens.

Brief description

Brightly coloured flowers with round leaves.

Dangers

Irate gardeners; pesticide sprays.

When to harvest

Leaves and flowers, summer to first frosts; seeds, late summer to first frosts.

Use in

Leaves and flowers in salads; leaves in stews; seeds as you would use capers. Pairs well with oily fish, fatty meats and strong-tasting mushrooms.

Fun fact

All nasturtiums descend from a couple of species native to Peru.

The almost circular leaves vary in size depending on growing conditions. Colours differ too, from a pale green to darker green, each with white veins radiating out from a central white dot. The long stems of each leaf grow out from the other side of this dot. There are different species, from bushy or dwarf *Tropaeolum minus*, which grow in a higgledy-piggledy ball-shape, to climbers such as *T. majus*. You're far more likely to end up foraging the climbers, as these are the ones that trail out of people's gardens.

Please note, it is legal to forage plants that grow onto public land. However, use some common sense and think about the owner. You may be removing the only colour in an otherwise barren garden. And remember, it is illegal to uproot any plant without permission. The patches I forage are from nasturtiums that have clearly grown out of a garden into public space and will definitely not be missed.

All the aerial parts of the plant are edible; leaves and flowers make an excellent addition to salads. Since nasturtiums have such a strong flavour, they can be added to soups and stews, replacing mustard. You can preserve both the leaves and the seeds (see recipe opposite). To preserve the leaves simply chop up finely and place in an ice cube tray. Then fill the gaps with a little olive oil, pressing down on the leaves to reduce any air pockets. Use when you want to give a bit of a kick to a stew or soup. You can stir in with mash or pasta, place onto a pizza, or mix with nasturtium capers (see opposite), vinegar and lemon juice to make a simple vinaigrette.

Nasturtium capers

The seeds of the nasturtium make an excellent, if not superior, substitute for capers. Check beneath the flowers and leaves of plants for the seeds in late summer. I love just how easily they roll off into a bag.

Ingredients

600g/1lb 5oz green nasturtium seeds
50g/1¾oz salt
500ml/18fl oz filtered or unchlorinated water (see page 71)
250ml/9fl oz white vinegar
5g/1 teaspoon brown sugar
5g/1 teaspoon black peppercorns
5g/1 teaspoon mustard or wild garlic seeds
4 dill sprigs

Method

Boil half a cup's worth of the water and stir in the salt until fully dissolved. Rinse the nasturtiums and put them into a jar. Cover with water and weigh the seeds down so they don't float. Leave for 2-3 days until they are just fermenting. A small amount of water from a previous ferment will help this process. Cover with a small piece of cloth and put a saucer beneath the jar to prevent unsightly spillages.

Drain and rinse the seeds. Scrub and rinse the jar and then return the seeds to the jar. In a saucepan, bring the vinegar to a gentle boil and stir in the sugar until fully dissolved. Allow to cool.

Add the rest of the ingredients to the jar. Seal and place in the fridge. Leave for 2 weeks and eat within 3 months.

OREGON GRAPE

Berberis x hortensis has deep green leaves and long, scented flowers.

The small, purple/ black fruits are carried in clusters like grapes.

The leaves can look like holly. Flowering time can vary, but usually between March and May.

Oregon grape

Berberis aquifolium
(syn. *Mahonia aquifolium*)

This is another non-native plant, originally introduced in the nineteenth century and prized for game cover. There are a few varieties of *Berberis*, and they vary in height; the tallest, *B. haematocarpa* or Mexican barberry, can grow up to around 3.6 metres (12 feet) tall.

The most common is the Oregon grape, *B. aquifolium*, likely to be a hybrid, which flowers and fruits in abundance giving it an advantage. This means it has gone rogue, happily naturalising in some places, but unhappily becoming invasive in others, with shrubs sometimes dominating a woodland understorey.

Urban dwellers will often find it in supermarket car parks, on roundabouts or as part of municipal planting schemes when some cover is required. A popular garden plant, you'll also find escapees along grass verges in suburban areas. It can be found across the British Isles, especially in the Midlands. It is sparse in the north of Scotland and almost non-existent outside cities in Northern Ireland.

AT A GLANCE

Where they grow

Woodland understorey; car parks; municipal planting.

Brief description

Holly-like plant with yellow flowers and clusters of blue-black berries.

Lookalikes

Holly, but holly leaves are alternate, and the berries are red and not in clusters.

Dangers

Avoid if pregnant or have an overactive thyroid. Has a laxative affect; too much can cause vomiting and lower blood pressure.

When to harvest

Flowers in spring; berries in summer.

Use in

To flavour and colour ice cream; in cordials. Berries can be eaten raw but are better cooked. Dried berries can be used like raisins.

Fun fact

Bears love Oregon grapes; trackers know when autumn is coming when their scat is full of berries!

It is an evergreen shrub with glossy, spiky leaves, similar in texture and shape to holly leaves. However, holly leaves are irregularly spaced along the stem of the tree and Oregon grape leaves grow in opposite pairs (pinnate).

The size of the overall shrub can vary tremendously; some plants will barely reach knee height while others can grow up to 1.8 metres (6 feet) tall. The bright yellow flowers bloom in the spring and can be used to flavour drinks.

When the Oregon grape fruits from early summer onwards, it is easy to harvest as the blue-black berries grow in dense clusters along long stems. The berries are at their best when they have a white sheen. Simply run your hand along the stem and strip off the fruit. The berries provide valuable food for small mammals and so I'll never strip a whole plant. If you don't find enough, then it's best to move on.

Pheasant berry

Himalayan honeysuckle

Leycesteria formosa

Our family name for this plant is 'toffee berry', I've also heard it called cheesecake berry. It's another one of those 'wow' plants because the berries really do taste like toffee or the finest treacle tart. They are far sweeter than most things you'll find in the wild.

You can eat them straight off the bush, but make sure to harvest at the right time or they will taste really unpleasant – a mixture of petrol and the bitterness of fernet, the Italian digestif used to temper the sweetest of cocktails.

Originally cultivated, it is starting to naturalise thanks to our avian friends. It can be found across the UK and in Ireland. Avoid foraging it from gardens; instead search in forests and on pieces of land around urban developments. It seems to tolerate a variety of conditions and I suspect it will continue to spread.

It grows to 2 metres (6 feet) and there is nothing quite like it. The flowers – which hang from tall, thin green canes – are

AT A GLANCE

Where they grow

Woodland margins; damp places; on the outskirts of urban areas.

Brief description

Tall plant with distinctive flowers and leaves.

Lookalikes

Some suggest fuchsia, which is also edible.

Conservation notes

Can become a valuable source of food for birds, but they will often beat you to the berries anyway.

When to harvest

Summer to first frost.

Use in

Eat raw or in puddings.

Fun fact

In India, children make toy flutes from the hollow stems, which is perhaps why the plant is sometimes known as 'whistle stick'.

PHEASANT BERRY
The flowers have large purple-red bracts which remain as the fruit ripens.
Berries turn from deep red-purple to almost black when ripe.
Leaves are oval-shaped and end in a point.

drooping clusters of individual pale white-pink flowers. Surrounding the flowers are large, pointed protective leaf-like structures in a purple-red, these are known as bracts. The canes will turn purple as the season progresses. Leaves are oval-shaped and end in a point.

The berries are also oval-shaped, with a neat, ornate little tail growing out of the end. There are three signs that the berries are ripe. Firstly, the tail will turn from red to a darker brown. Next, the berry will turn from dark red/purple to almost black. Lastly, the berry will become squashy.

Frozen yoghurt with Himalayan honeysuckle ripple

Most plants will only have a small handful of berries that are ripe at any one time; we just snack on them, but you could collect them and freeze as you go. They lose their integrity a little after that but they work as a purée, such as in this frozen yoghurt ripple recipe inspired by a similar one in Adele Nozedar's excellent book, *The Garden Forager*.

Ingredients

For the frozen yoghurt:

2 large egg yolks
1 large egg
50g/1¾oz golden caster sugar
5g/1 teaspoon cornflour
300ml/10fl oz whole milk
Grated zest of 1 small unwaxed lemon
2.5ml/½ teaspoon vanilla essence
250g/9oz Greek yoghurt

For the Himalayan honeysuckle-berry purée:

115g/4oz Himalayan honeysuckle berries, washed
30g/1oz golden caster sugar
15ml/1 tablespoon water

Method

Whisk together the egg yolks, egg, sugar and cornflour in large bowl until it forms a paste.

Gently heat the milk with the lemon zest. Keep a careful eye on it and as soon as it is about to come to a boil (when it starts to froth up) remove from the heat and add the paste and vanilla essence. Keep stirring until it thickens then set aside to cool.

Beat in the yoghurt and freeze for 2 hours.

Next, to make the purée, put the berries, sugar and water into a pan. Mash down with a wooden spoon so the juice bursts out of the berries. Heat gently and keep stirring until the sugar has fully dissolved. Once it has, push the contents of the pan through a sieve.

Take the yoghurt mixture out of the fridge and stir vigorously. The trick is to break up any ice crystals and create a smooth paste. Gently pour in the purée as you stir, you might need a friend to help here to get this bit right. Ideally, you want the purée to swirl through the yoghurt so that it looks as fancy as possible. Enjoy!

Pine

Pinus spp.

Pine has a lemony scent that might remind you of toilet cleaner, cannabis, lemon peel or craft ale – depending on your frame of reference. The smell comes from a mixture of organic compounds known as terpenes, which are thought to act as a pine tree's natural defence; it is true that they can act as antivirals, antifungals and insecticides.

However, terpenes are also thought to have a secondary function, and one that might account for the age of pine trees in evolutionary terms. Terpenes are very volatile; they rise up from the trees and bond to the oxygen and free radicals in the air. Together these create an aerosol and aerosols will combine to form clouds. In other words, the smell of pine trees enables them to create their own water supply.

Clouds formed in this way are much brighter than clouds that bond with pollution. If you have ever seen a blue haze over a forest, this is the aerosols being dispersed by the sun, hence the name of the Blue Ridge mountains in Virginia.

These light and volatile scents mean that pine is a great food. Most of the tree can be

AT A GLANCE

Where they grow

Parks; roadsides; riversides; woodlands.

Brief description

Tall trees with ovoid cones and needles.

Lookalikes

Yew; Norfolk Island pine.

Dangers

High quantities of terpenes can be poisonous. Mistaking for a yew. Ponderosa and lollypop pine have poisoned cattle.

Conservation notes

Only pull off the needles that you need. Never peel bark from around the trunk; wait for branches to fall or be lopped.

When to harvest

Needles in the spring; nuts in autumn; pollen mid-spring; pollen cones early–mid-spring.

Use in

Nuts toasted in salads and Mediterranean dishes; needles to flavour vinegars; infused in tea; beer; cordials; dried.

PINE
Young pollen-bearing
male cone.
Mature female cone.
The bark
is a scaly
orange-
brown.
Needles grow in
groups of between
two and five.

used. Even the inner layer of the bark can be peeled and eaten as a starch substitute. I like the flavour and have them fried like chips, but some find it terrible. American forager Steve Brill calls it 'a survival food for dire emergencies'. The small pollen cones are also edible, but equally divisive. I love to eat them as a wayside snack throughout late spring. Every pine tree will also produce nuts. Some are too small to bother with, others are better than shop-bought pine nuts.

Pine trees are pretty easy to identify. Look for long evergreen needles in bunches of one to five. (Spruce has smaller, flatter needles.) Their woody cones have overlapping scales that open when the weather is fine. They can grow up to 55 metres (180 feet) tall, with other species being much smaller, shrub-like trees.

Pine needle vinegar

This works very well with just one species of pine, but if you really want it to shine then use as many different pine needles as you can find. I also spruce mine up with some spruce tips. In early spring, the trees in one of the parks in a nearby town get a trim. This means I can pick up a lovely selection of conifers. Before you do this, make sure to familiarise yourself with yew trees, Norfolk Island pines and ponderosa pines, all of which are poisonous, and only one of which is actually a pine.

Ingredients

Pine (and spruce, if using) needles
Apple cider vinegar (or white vinegar if unavailable)

Method

Cut the ends off your needles, clean them and then pat dry. Place inside a container to just over half way and top up with vinegar. Cover with a piece of cloth and an elastic band, then put it at the back of your cupboard and forget about it for about 3-6 weeks.

Strain into a clean bottle and use as you would normal vinegar. It works as a substitute for strong-tasting balsamic vinegar in dishes.

Pine needle tea

I love this drink and make it once a year, in the late spring, when the needles are at their best. In Korea, where the recipe originates, only the Korean red pine is used. In honour of this, I also like to use a single pine, a Scots pine that grows at the bottom of the hill where I live.

Ingredients

850ml/1½ pints filtered or unchlorinated water (see page 71)
115g/4oz honey or sugar
115g/4oz pine needles

Method

Boil the water before stirring in the honey or sugar and then stir until fully dissolved. Allow to cool.

Cut the sharp points and the woody ends from the pine needles and place inside a clean jar. Pour the water solution over the needles and leave in a warmish spot in sunlight (a windowsill is ideal). Cover with a piece of material or a tea towel to keep out any dust or flies.

After 5 days, a few bubbles will start to form on the top and around the needles, and at this point it is ready to drink, although I leave mine for a little bit longer to make a drier drink.

Once it has brewed to your satisfaction it can be refrigerated and drunk within a month or so. You will need to vent the gas every now and then as your pine needle tea will continue to ferment.

Once ready, it is consumed cold and served diluted like a cordial. I like mine at a ratio of 2:1, although you can dilute it further to taste depending on how sweet your tooth is.

PINEAPPLE WEED

The leaves are finely divided and feathery. Flowers appear from May to November.

Pineapple weed has a cone-like head filled with tightly packed petal-less flowers.

Pineapple weed

Matricaria discoidea

Pineapple weed was introduced to Britain in the nineteenth century and quickly spread around the country. The rise of the motorcar is supposed to have helped carry it even further due to sticky rubber tyres.

Pineapple weed is easy to identify: the leaves resemble the feathery foliage of camomile. The flowers are rather unusual too, comprising clusters of tiny, yellow-green balls. If you find something that fits this description, crush it and sniff it: do you get pineapple, perhaps with a hint of camomile?

My kids love making drinks in the summer months. They gather pineapple weed, place the flower heads in hot water, stir in some sugar, allow the water to cool, and then strain off the liquid.

Pineapple weed is often drunk as a tea by country-dwellers in North America. A few flower heads infused in hot water for 3–5 minutes makes a very agreeable herbal tea. But many also cite its use as a traditional remedy for ailments such as insomnia, fatigue, constipation and bloating.

AT A GLANCE

Where they grow

Field margins; beside footpaths and roads.

Brief description

Up to 20cm/8in tall. Yellow-green petal-less flowers; smell of pineapple when crushed.

Lookalikes

Camomile, scented mayweed – but both have petals.

Dangers

Pollution and traffic on roadsides. Avoid if pregnant.

When to harvest

May–November.

Use in

As a tea, cordial or ice lolly.

Fun fact

Pineapple weed is an effective insect repellent, and was commonly used by the Blackfeet Nation and Indigenous peoples in North America.

RASPBERRY
Wild berries can vary in size.
Raspberries flower from June-August.
The leaves comprise 3-7 leaflets.
Berries appear from June-September.

Raspberry

Rubus spp.

It can be a delightful moment when you discover raspberries growing in the wild, although the size of your haul can vary greatly. One summer I searched a nearby 18-hectare (45-acre) wild area, certain I would return with a rich bounty, and instead all I found were three tiny berries. The same year, in Scotland, I stumbled across a loch that was totally surrounded by delicious yellow raspberries. The right conditions meant the canes had spread and produced a bumper harvest.

Ten years on, and due to ash die back, it looks like there will be richer pickings at my local site. The extra light has meant the canes have spread, basking in the sunshine as the tree canopy has dwindled.

Raspberry canes grow upwards, kinking slightly at the top. They are all looking for a passing tree or shrub to rest on. In the second year, each cane will start to spread out and the crop will increase. Typically, you'll find first- and second-year canes in one area. Pigeons can be a problem and in some spots you do have to beat them to it.

AT A GLANCE

Where they grow

Woodlands; garden and allotment escapee; footpaths; roadsides; loch sides.

Brief description

Looks like a red blackberry and is usually smaller.

Lookalikes

Possibly an unripe blackberry.

Dangers

Avoid raspberry leaf tea in first trimester of pregnancy. Avoid older leaves altogether as the cyanide content increases.

When to harvest

Leaves, spring–summer; berries, June–September.

Use in

Leaves for herbal tea. Fruit raw, in puddings, beverage infusions. Pairs well with basil, tomato, black olives, passion fruit, cinnamon, asparagus, stone fruits.

Fun fact

You can get red, purple, gold and black varieties of raspberry.

I've made cocktails pairing basil with raspberries and they are quite delicious. Either make using a basil-infused vodka, or muddle basil leaves with raspberries in the bottom of a shaker, then fill with vodka and ice. Serve with a club soda, or neat, depending on how your day has been.

Raspberry leaves can also be used to make a tea that is said to help to induce labour and encourage milk production, but should be avoided in the first trimester. Always consult a medical professional before use. We also share raspberries with other creatures. Check the leaves for mining moths and carefully examine each berry as you pick. There are a variety of maggots that like to call them home. The later it is in the season, the higher the chances of finding them. If you do, you have a choice: pick them out, or find a better crop. But always remember: it was the maggot's home long before you came along.

Rosebay willowherb

Fireweed

Epilobium angustifolium (syn. *Chamerion angustifolium*)

If you happen to find yourself looking out the window of a train heading cross-country on a late summer's day, you might notice flashes of purple as you speed along. The likelihood is that it's rosebay willowherb, a much overlooked wild plant that is commonly found across Europe, East Asia and historically also in the Americas.

The plant took a while to settle in the UK and is absent from the texts of ancient herbalists. However, following the Great Fire of London in 1666 it apparently started growing more abundantly: this plant relishes the bare soil left in the wake of devastation.

Still, it remained rather elusive for many years after that, and certainly wasn't as ubiquitous as it is now. Then came the land clearance necessitated by construction of the Victorian railway system that still criss-crosses our country, and the road network that followed. Both helped to spread these beautiful plants across our verdant country.

AT A GLANCE

Where they grow

Woodland; uncultivated land; mountainsides; river banks; roadsides; railway sidings.

Brief description

Up to 1.5m/5ft tall. Flowers purple; leaves spear-shaped.

Lookalikes

Himalayan balsam; great willowherb.

Dangers

Causes an allergic reaction in some (see main text). Sedatives, antipyretics or laxatives can be amplified with use. Habitual use is dangerous to the liver.

When to harvest

Leaves, shoots and roots in spring; stem and flowers in summer.

Use in

Leaves as a tea substitute; flowers in jellies and drinks; pith as a wayside snack.

Fun fact

Following the Second World War, it became known as bombweed as it was the first plant to appear on the many bombsites.

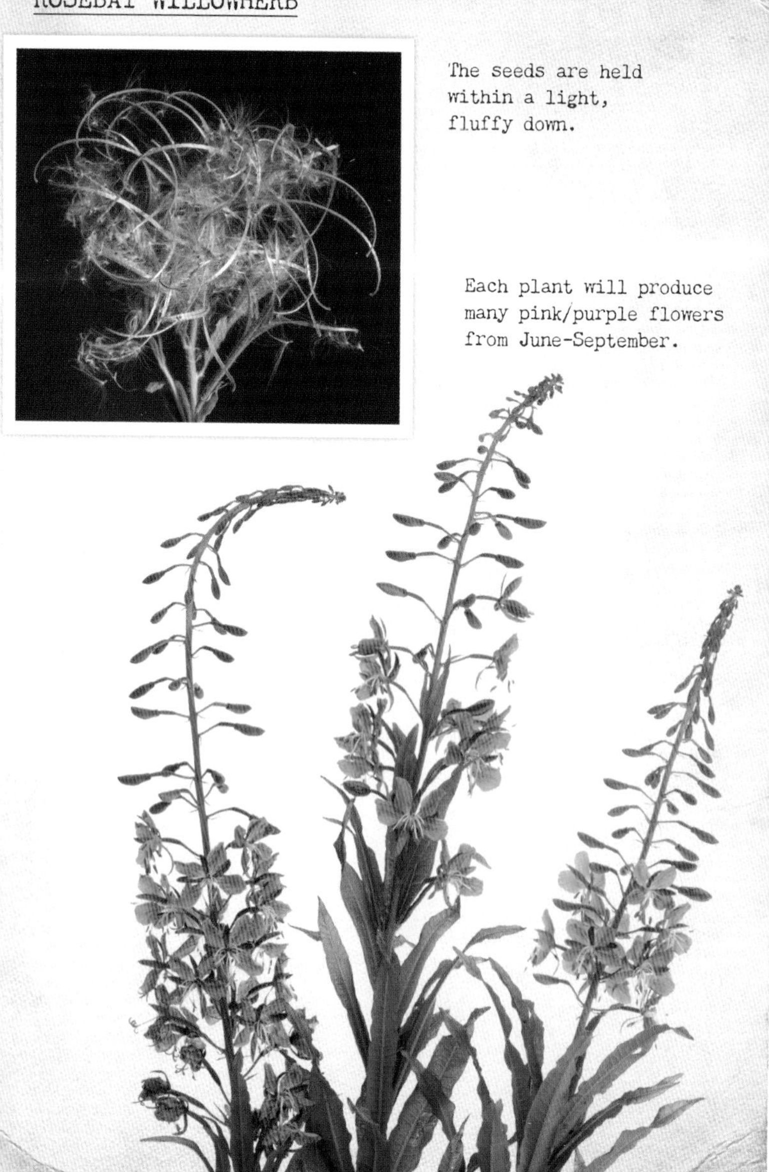
ROSEBAY WILLOWHERB
The seeds are held within a light, fluffy down.
Each plant will produce many pink/purple flowers from June-September.

There is an ever-growing patch of rosebay willowherb on the edge of a path near one of my daily foraging haunts. Huge clouds of fluffy seeds fill the air between August and September. During this time, if you see a plume of seeds, follow it to its source and you may find your own patch of willowherb.

Other distinguishing features help explain how the herb got its name. The number of petals might differ, but the colour is at least similar to the wild rose (*Rosa rugosa*). Some insist its leaves resemble willow leaves, while others say bay – so it looks as if the plant has been named by committee and everyone is happy.

The plants are rather sociable and grow in patches rather than as single plants. Look out for the tall flowering spikes with many blooms facing in all directions, all propped up on a large stem. Spear-shaped green leaves with a white rib in the centre grow in a spiral formation up its stem. Often, when in flower, you'll see many seed pods forming beneath. They are an artist's dream, with one side green and the other more pinkish. When they are ready, they split open and fill the air with seeds.

I've offered the petals raw to many people and subsequently found that a very small proportion (1 in 2,000) experience a scratchy throat. Eat sparingly at first to find out if you are one of the unlucky ones who may be a little allergic to this plant. If not, then there are a few uses for this most striking of wild flowers.

Firstly, find a plant that has flowered but not gone to seed. Split the stem open and pull out the white inner part. Some use this for stews and soups, but in reality you'll probably just snack on it now and then – taste-wise, it is a bit like cucumber with a peppery aftertaste.

If you don't fancy eating pith – which is fair enough – try the flowers. You can make a great drink with them. Half-fill a 1-litre (1¾-pint) container with the flowers, pour over boiling water, add the juice of half a lemon then let it sit overnight. You might want to put a tea towel or a piece of cloth over the top to stop flies getting in. I also dry the flowers on a hot day, spreading them out on a tray and leaving it in the sun. These can then be used to flavour cocktails, jellies and sorbets.

Lastly, there's the tea. I used to make this simply by drying the leaves. I tied up bundles of them and hung them somewhere out of direct sunlight where air could circulate around them, and then stored them in a tin, using them like regular tea leaves. Many of my foraging friends were also fermenting them to make a traditional Russian tea called Ivan tea.

Ivan tea

Pick only healthy looking leaves; discard any that are turning brown or have been nibbled. If you can take your time doing this on a warm day, it is a very mindful activity and will help you unwind. Place a tea towel or a sheet of newspaper on a flat surface and pile the leaves on top. Leave for at least 12 and up to 24 hours. You want them to be dry enough to bend in the middle without breaking. Test a few by folding in half.

Next for some more mindfulness! Roll up each leaf between your palms. When rolled put them into a clean jar; don't pack them in, you need a bit of air around them. Once the jar is filled with your rolled up leaves, cover with a small piece of cloth and secure with a piece of twine, string or an elastic band and leave on your work surface. You can add some of the dried flowers for extra flavour. Any kind of dried edible flower can be used, roses make good candidates.

Give the contents of the jar a mix every now and then. The fermentation process takes about 2-5 days depending on the local conditions. It's worth trying a brew after two days just to see what it tastes like. You are looking for fruity and floral flavours and aromas; the herbal smell should dissipate.

Next, you need to halt fermentation by drying. If it is 30°C (86°F) or more outside, you can dry in the garden. Again, place on a tray, and put somewhere where kids or cats won't knock it over! On cooler days, dry in the oven on the lowest temperature with the door wedged open to allow evaporation (see page 87). Or, if you are very keen, use a dehydrator. The leaves will be ready when they are totally dry.

Allow to cool, then store, use and serve just as you would regular tea leaves - with or without milk and sugar.

Rose

Rosa spp.

The rose is one of the most common plants in both the ornamental garden and the hedgerow. It is planted in the former to tempt people in, and in the latter to keep them out.

Wild or cultivated, they are all of interest to the forager, and are one of the few wild plants that can be used all year round. The variety of cultivated roses means that, especially in southern England, blooms are often found from spring right through to the depths of winter. Then there are the rose hips; forming in the later summer they can cling on all through winter and into spring.

It's worth trying out a few different rose petals, as there are different flavours and textures available. Some add texture to a salad and a hint of floweriness. Others will overpower and are better used in an infusion. I especially like adding a few rose petals to a gin and then making a flowery Tom Collins.

You can also add flavour to more than just cocktails by making some gulkand – a rose petal sugar. Place layer upon layer of icing sugar and particularly fragrant rose petals

AT A GLANCE

Where they grow

Gardens; parks; hedgerows; shorelines.

Brief description

Various cultivated flower types growing from a thorned shrub. Flowers become hips in late summer/autumn.

Lookalikes

Peonies; gardenias.

Dangers

Cultivated roses are often sprayed with nasty chemicals, so avoid very pristine-looking flowers. If using the hips, carefully remove or strain out the seeds and seed coating. They are not edible and can be an irritant.

When to harvest

Petals, spring/summer; hips, autumn/winter.

Fun fact

Roses grown in space smell better than those on earth. Adapting to their surroundings, they produce less volatile oils but the ones they do produce are more fragrant.

ROSE
Harvest the bright red hips in autumn and winter.
Wild roses vary in colour.
Wild roses have five petals and many yellow stamens.

inside a jar. You can add fennel, cardamom seeds and honey between each layer too. Use double the weight of sugar to petals.

When full, place the jar on a windowsill in full sun. The volume will decrease over time, so keep adding layers of sugar and petals each day until the jar is full and changes in volume no longer occur. This will take about a week. Then shake daily and leave for about two months. The result is a rose petal jam that you can use to flavour milkshakes, puddings and a champion Victoria sponge – it will open up a whole new world of flavour possibilities.

Later in the year you'll have the rose hips. My favourite use for these is a recipe by Fergus Drennan. He would boil up the hips until soft, strain and use the liquid as a somewhat unusual, but nevertheless delicious, stock for beetroot soup.

Staghorn sumac

Rhus typhina

If you are wondering where the name 'staghorn sumac' comes from, stand back from a tree and look at how it grows from a distance. The hairy branches reach upwards like a stag's antlers.

Although it is not a native tree, it can spread. I've seen new sucker growth radiating out from the original tree and covering an area the size of a tennis court.

Predominantly, it grows in and around the UK's major cities, including Edinburgh, Glasgow and Belfast. Mostly, you'll only find staghorn sumac (*Rhus typhina*) and possibly smooth sumac (*R. glabra*). There are poisonous sumacs, but I've only ever seen one growing in a neighbour's garden. Poison sumac (*Toxicodendron vernix*) is mainly found in the south-eastern states of the USA. This has drooping clusters of white berries rather than the upward-pointing berries of edible sumacs.

From around late August onwards, you'll be able to harvest this tree's unusual fruit. The clusters of dry, hairy red berries may not

AT A GLANCE

Where they grow

Spreading out from urban and suburban gardens.

Brief description

Tree with furry wood and antler-like branches.

Lookalikes

Smooth sumac.

Dangers

Poison sumac – rare in the UK.

Conservation notes

Considered a non-native invasive species, so harvest away but please leave some for other foragers.

When to harvest

Late summer.

Use in

As a drink or as a lemon flavouring.

Fun fact

The leaves of sumac are used as an ingredient of black ink.

STAGHORN SUMAC
The fruits form red furry clusters.
The ground powder can be used to make za'atar, a Middle Eastern spice blend.
The branches of this tree look like stag's antlers.

look or sound too appetising, but if you pick one and nibble it, you'll find it has a strong taste of lemon – or rather the citric acid tang of lemons.

The berries can be infused in cold water overnight to create a lemonade-type drink. Just take a few clusters and infuse in a litre/1¾ pints of cold water, adding a teaspoon of honey to taste.

You can also make sumac spice, which requires a little bit more effort but is worth the extra work. First, rinse the berry clusters in water, dry them in the sun (or use an oven or dehydrator). Next, pluck each berry off the cluster, and then either whizz in a blender or crush with a pestle and mortar. Pass through a sieve with a bowl underneath; what you collect in the bowl is your spice. Use as a rub, a marinade, to spice up a salad or mix with equal parts of toasted, ground cumin seeds, sesame and dried oregano to make your very own za'atar blend.

STINGING
NETTLE
It is the fine hairs on the leaves that will sting you.
The heart-shaped leaves are jagged and toothed.

Stinging nettle

Urtica dioica

I was about seven or eight years old when I found a recipe asking for 'young nettle tops'. It was late in the season and the nettles were starting to flower. It was the first recipe I'd ever followed and I wanted to make sure I did so exactly. In my young mind, this meant picking the right quantity and overlooking the fact that book emphasised – *young* nettles. The resulting dish was vile, gritty and unappetising: an early lesson about harvesting food at the right time.

Nettles will die back during the winter months and grow again from a thick root that spreads through nutrient-rich soil in the late winter to early spring. You'll find them growing on woodland edges and clearings, on field boundaries, river banks, in damp areas and all over allotments. They especially like areas that have been manured.

Nettles can grow very tall. There is a footpath near Glastonbury with nettles so high they have stung me on my eyelids and ears. The hairy leaves have jagged edges ending in a point; it's the hairs that'll get you.

AT A GLANCE

Where they grow

Recovering land; damp places; recently disturbed ground. Likes nutrient-rich soil.

Brief description

Jagged, heart-shaped leaves that grow in opposite pairs up a central stem. Can grow up to 2m/6½ft by the end of the season, but are often much smaller. Fine hairs on stems and leaves that sting when touched.

Lookalikes

Dead-nettles and other members of the mint family. Look for fine hairs that sting to differentiate.

Dangers

Being stung! Also, older nettles contain calcium oxalate crystals, which can cause kidney problems.

When to harvest

Spring and autumn.

Fun fact

Nettlecloth became a catch-all term for any fine material in Scotland, as sheets and tablecloths were frequently made from nettles.

The best time to pick nettles is in the spring and again in the autumn. After that they thicken up, turn a darker green and the sting becomes more vicious when they are going to seed.

Some people pick with a bag and scissors, others a knife and a glove, and the brave (or stupid) claim they can flatten the tiny stingy hairs with a firm grasp and then pluck the nettle tops. I tend to use gloves and bag; even with a lifetime of picking, I always sting myself. Some foragers like to be stung and claim it staves off rheumatism.

Whichever picking method you choose, always go for the top 6–10 leaves of a plant that is standing tall and erect. That means it isn't yet flowering – the weight of the flowers and seeds causes the plant to droop. It is good to check the undersides of the leaves. There are a number of native butterflies, including the tortoiseshell, which lay eggs around the same time we harvest nettles. These look like tiny, brightly coloured and tightly clustered balls that cling to the underside of the leaf.

A very simple nettle soup

This simple recipe is a great introduction to exploring the world of wild food cuisine. It's been adapted so that even the most terrified of cooks can follow it. If it is your first year of foraging, try this recipe - it's where I started!

Ingredients

400g/14oz stinging nettle tops
1 litre/1¾ pints vegetable stock

Method

Wash the nettles, then cut into pieces with scissors or a knife. Boil 1 litre/1¾ pints of water and add a single vegetable stock cube. Stir until dissolved.

Throw in your chopped up nettles, turn down the heat and simmer for 2 mins. Put in a blender, blend for a few pulses, until the nettles are totally chopped up, and then serve.

A slightly more complicated version

The more experienced cook can opt for this version, which is richer and has more flavour.

Ingredients

15g/1 tablespoon butter or oil
1 medium onion
1 medium potato
1 litre/1¾ pints vegetable stock
400g/14oz stinging nettle tops
15ml/1 tablespoon cider (or pine needle) vinegar

Method

Heat up the butter or oil in a saucepan. Roughly chop the onion and potato. Fry them both, covered, until the onion has softened. This will take about 10-15 mins. Add the stock and simmer for a further 10 mins ensuring the potato is soft.

Wash your nettles, then cut them up into pieces with scissors or a knife and add them to the pot. Allow them to wilt by simmering for a further 2 mins, then blend as above.

Stir in the vinegar and season to taste.

Nettle spanakopita recipe

My old friend Lisa Cutcliffe happily shared this recipe with me. Lisa is an extraordinarily brilliant forager. The beauty of this recipe is that you can buy some of the wild ingredients in conventional food shops and either substitute or leave others out. If you make it every year, you can use it as an edible road map of how far you have progressed with your foraging. Enjoy a slice with a wild salad or as a great portable lunch. Serves 4-6.

Ingredients

50g/1¾oz smashed hazelnuts
50g/1¾oz walnut pieces
300g/10½oz nettle tops, washed, all stalks removed
100g/3½oz wild garlic leaves/buds
20g/¾oz unsalted butter, plus extra for frying
10g/2 teaspoons powdered seaweed, e.g. dulse or laver (optional)
20g/¾oz fresh seasonal or button mushrooms
6 eggs
50g/1¾oz Cheddar cheese
300g/3½oz feta
Dried wild marjoram (or oregano)
1 pack filo pastry
Olive or rapeseed oil
Freshly ground black pepper or ground alexanders
Cayenne pepper
Lemon juice or chopped lemon balm

Method

Toast the nuts in a dry pan and set aside.

Wilt the greens until no water is left, toss in the butter and 1 teaspoon powdered seaweed (if using), set aside

Sauté the mushrooms in a teaspoon of butter or oil and set aside.

Beat the eggs in a large bowl, add the nuts, cheeses, wilted greens, mushrooms and marjoram (or oregano).

Cut some baking paper slightly larger than an ovenproof skillet or heavy pan. Line the inside of the pan, brush the paper with olive or rapeseed oil, scrunch the paper up and then flatten it down again.

Lay the baking paper on a work surface and place the filo on top in multi-directional, overlapping layers, with the corners lying over the edges of the paper. Oil each layer as you go and season one layer with black pepper (or alexanders) and cayenne.

Place the paper and filo layers in the pan, easing it into the corners. Fill with the cheese and greens mixture, flatten out evenly.

Fold over the edges of the filo to create a lid, press down but leave the top a little ruffled; scatter with another teaspoon of seaweed powder (if using).

Preheat the oven to 200°C/180°C fan/400°F/gas 6. Cook the pie on the hob for 10 mins, then place in the oven for 20 mins (or until the tips of the pastry are golden). Allow to cool before cutting. Season with lemon juice or chopped lemon balm to taste.

Nettle cordial

Try this recipe for a simple cordial - when I make it, my kids always ask for more!

Ingredients

A saucepan full of nettles
1 litre/1¾ pints of water
350g/12oz sugar
30ml/2 tablespoons of lemon juice (optional)
1 stick of liquorice (optional)

Method

Heat the water and add the nettles. Simmer very gently until the water changes colour, strain and stir in the sugar and lemon juice (if using).

If you are the experimental type then you can have a go at adding some liquorice and less sugar.

Allow to cool then pour into a clean bottle.

Sweet chestnut

Castanea sativa

Sweet chestnuts can be found from St Ives to Inverness, across Wales and into Northern Ireland. The Romans can be thanked for bringing them over, although as with many trees in the UK, they are also deliberately planted.

Older trees are wondrous to behold. Living to a ripe old age of 700 years or more, with a girth that can measure over 2 metres (6.5 feet) in diameter, these are monstrous trees that look as if they have twisted their way up from another world. The fissures in the bark can be very deep. Of course, trees this size have to start somewhere, and often you'll find smaller, shrub-like examples in parks and gardens.

The deciduous leaves will sometimes grow to around 30 centimetres (12 inches) long. They have spiky, toothed edges and parallel veins. The clustered nuts sit in a spiky shell. They look very similar to conkers – the fruit of the horse chestnut (*Aesculus hippocastanum*) – only with many more spikes, and the nut has one flat(ish) side.

AT A GLANCE

Where they grow

Parks and gardens.

Brief description

Trees are tall, bearing clusters of nuts with spiky shells.

Lookalikes

Horse chestnut; buckeye.

Dangers

Being hit on the head by a falling nut.

Conservation notes

If you have space, plant one. Future generations of birds, insects and humans will thank you.

When to harvest

Late autumn.

Use in

Can be ground into flour and made into pasta; gives soups an extra dimension; as stuffing; simply roasted. Pairs with salty meats, spicy food and improves sprouts.

Fun fact

The Romans mainly used sweet chestnuts to make a flour.

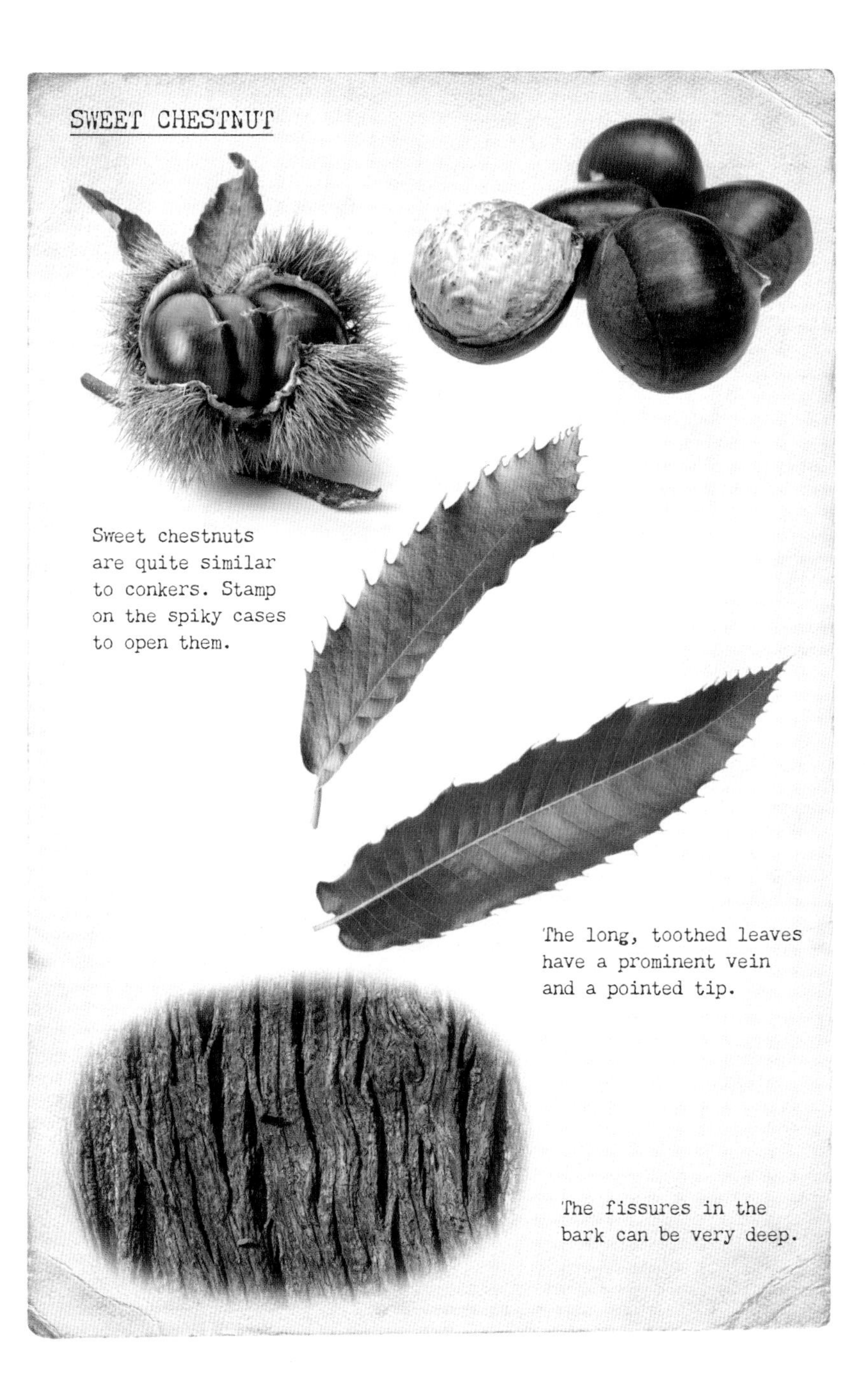

SWEET CHESTNUT

Sweet chestnuts are quite similar to conkers. Stamp on the spiky cases to open them.

The long, toothed leaves have a prominent vein and a pointed tip.

The fissures in the bark can be very deep.

Practice has shown that the only way to get the nuts out of their shells is to press on them heavily with the heel of a boot. Repeat until they pop out. I'm not sure if I'm getting smaller, but, over the years, the nuts seem to be getting bigger. This makes harvesting them far more worthwhile.

I like to de-shell them on site; it can be a real faff doing a load of them when you get home. Also, it means you can discard any that have holes in them – ensuring that the critters that made the holes remain in their natural habitat.

Chestnuts are prized by chefs, and therefore cookbooks and the internet are awash with recipes. Yet sometimes the simplest methods are the best. Just score an X-shaped hole in the shell of each one. This allows any gas build-up to escape and prevents the nut from exploding in your oven. Place your scored nuts on a baking tray and roast at 200°C/180°C fan/400°F/gas 6 for about 30 minutes.

Three-cornered leek

three-cornered garlic

Allium triquetrum

Three-cornered leek is slowly making its way across the world from its Mediterranean and Canary Island home. It can now be found in Japan, Oceania, USA, Canada, Argentina and South Africa. In the UK, it's working its way up from southern England into Scotland, Wales and Northern Ireland. It always amazes me just how tasty many of our introduced and invasive plants are. Three-cornered leek is no exception.

This plant can out-compete native species and is considered so invasive that it is an offence to spread it into the wild. It may sound strange to say it, as it should be embedded into the mindset of foragers to only uproot plants with permission, but many advocate ripping this plant out of the ground completely and using the bulbs in place of onions. In this respect they are great pickled.

All that being said, this is a pretty little plant and reminiscent of a white bluebell, but with a green vein running down the

AT A GLANCE

Where they grow

Disturbed ground; hedgerows; riverbanks; woodland; roadsides; gardens.

Brief description

Looks like a snowdrop or white bluebell, but with green veins in the centre of each petal.

Lookalikes

Snowdrops; white bluebells; bluebells before flowering.

Dangers

Confusing with bluebells; pesticide sprays.

Conservation notes

Considered invasive, so pick away and don't replant.

When to harvest

March–May (late winter in Cornwall).

Use in

Flowers as a garnish; bulbs as onions; stems and leaves in place of spring onions.

Fun fact

Three-cornered leek was introduced to Britain in the 1700s and took 100 years to become naturalised.

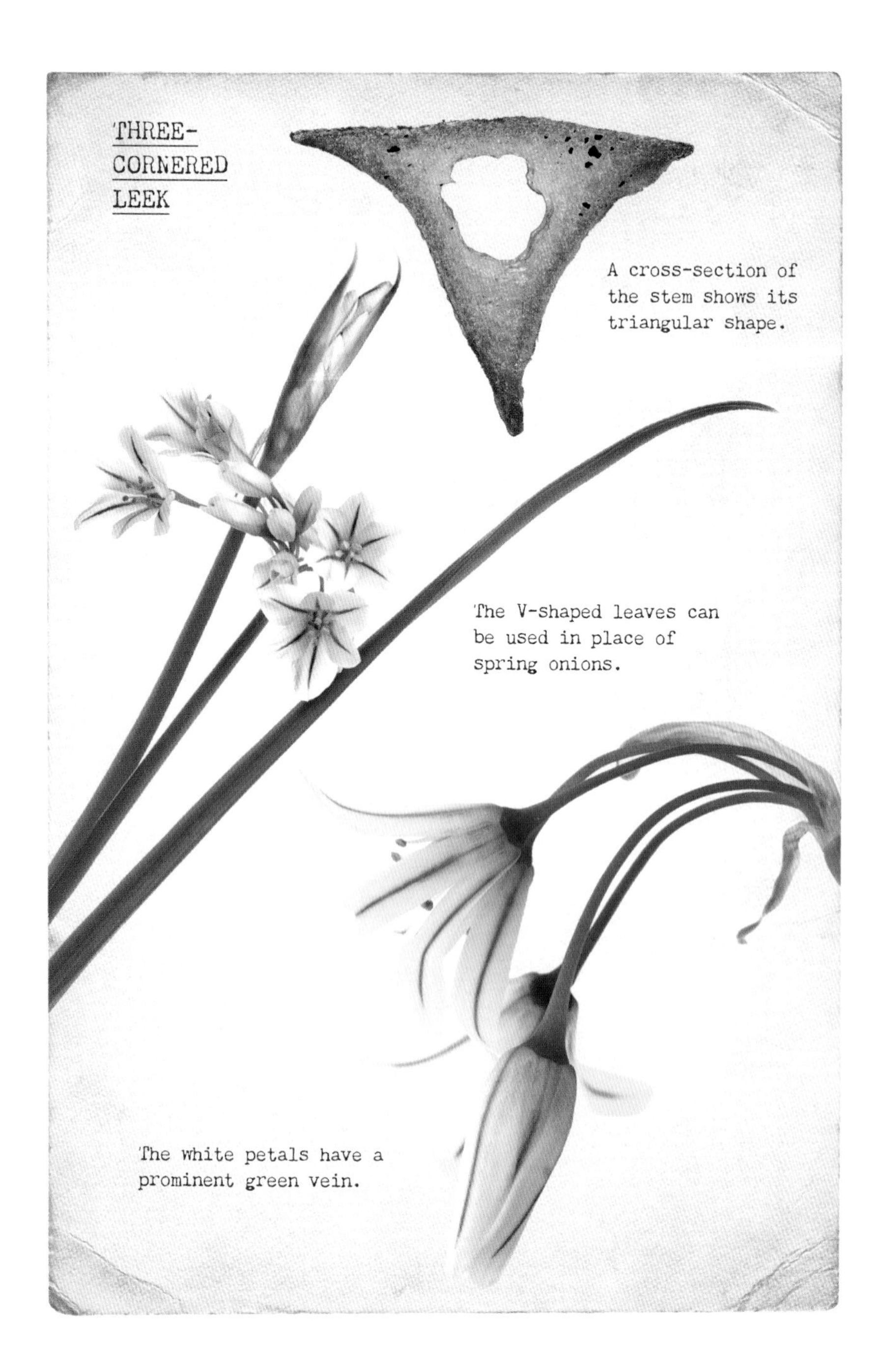
THREE-
CORNERED
LEEK
A cross-section of the stem shows its triangular shape.
The V-shaped leaves can be used in place of spring onions.
The white petals have a prominent green vein.

middle of each flower petal. Pluck a leaf and you'll notice that it is V-shaped. If you are worried you've picked a bluebell by mistake, then snap the bottom of the leaf; if it's rounded it is a bluebell, but if it is V-shaped and smells of onions you are okay. Pick one leaf at a time rather than grabbing a large number so you don't pull up bluebell leaves by mistake.

Use the bulbs in place of onions in a dish or the leaves and stems in place of spring onions. A friend of mine loves the flowers fried in butter and then sprinkled over savoury dishes. Stalks also work well as a garnish on fish and the flowers and leaves are excellent on scrambled eggs.

WALNUT

Ripe walnuts.

The nuts will often fall out of their husks.

Young walnuts developing on a branch.

Walnut

Juglans spp.

I can remember the first time I foraged a walnut. I was standing on a rooftop terrace in Romania in the 1990s and I leaned forward and grabbed a nut from a tree growing in the abundant garden below. I couldn't believe what I was picking was a walnut; its green husk looked nothing like the nuts we would have in a bowl at Christmas time. Then I noticed a crack in the husk and tore it open to find a walnut.

There are about 21 species of walnut, but in the UK you are only likely to come across two varieties: Persian/Common walnut (*Juglans regia*) and Black walnut (*Juglans nigra*). They are mostly found south of the Pennines, although I know of at least three people who are actively planting them across Scotland and the north in preparation for rising temperatures.

I love the way the walnut grows. New growth never seems to go in the same direction; starting from horizontal, each branch will, season by season, start to point upwards. After a while the branches will look like the antlers on an old stag.

AT A GLANCE

Where they grow

Where there is room; often in parks, gardens and on old country estates; on the edges of woods.

Brief description

Large, wide-spreading tree.

Lookalikes

Pecan, edible and extremely uncommon in the UK. Possibly chestnut, also edible.

Dangers

Windfall nuts falling out of the tree.

When to harvest

Sap in spring; green walnuts in summer; mature nuts in autumn.

Use in

Green walnuts can be pickled; mature ones can be used for baking or to flavour wine. Pairs well with cakes, tart fruits, aged cheese and goat's cheese.

Fun fact

Its decorative and hard-wearing wood is used for furniture and even guitar fretboards.

The trees are large and deciduous with pale grey bark. The feather-like leaflets grow in 5–9 pairs along a central stem with a single leaf at the end. Trees can grow up to 30 metres (100 feet) tall and they spread to about 15 metres (50 feet) wide. If you have room to plant a lovely big walnut tree please do – future generations will love you for it.

Each year I dry out a few leaves for our annual winter party. I use a single leaf from the leaflet in our mulled wine – it adds a tannic richness to the cheapest of reds. In the autumn, the green outer husk will split and the perfectly ripe nuts will start to fall off the tree.

Pickled green walnuts

You can also harvest walnuts in early summer. Wait until they are about the size of a ping-pong ball, then pluck off the tree and pierce them with a knife or skewer; if you don't feel any resistance, then they are good. If you do feel resistance then I'm afraid they have gone over and you'll have to wait until next year. You can still use them in nocino (see page 146), but you won't be able to pickle them. Some people wear gloves when doing this to stop their hands becoming stained with the juice from the husk. In fact, throughout this whole process the juice can stain, so it might be wise to wear gloves and an apron.

Ingredients

2 litres/3½ pints water
200g/7oz salt
2kg/4lb 8oz green walnuts
100ml/3½fl oz elderflower wine (or dry white wine)
500ml/18fl oz elderflower wine vinegar (or white wine vinegar)
100ml/3½fl oz pine needle and spruce vinegar (or balsamic)

30g/2 tablespoons brown sugar
1 thumb of wood avens/clove root (or three cloves)
10 coriander seeds (optional)
20 peppercorns
1 cinnamon stick
10g/2 teaspoons mustard seeds

Method

Boil up the water and stir in the salt. Allow the brine to cool and pour into a large bowl or tub.

Next, pierce each walnut about three times with a fork. This helps the walnuts to absorb the brine, and later the vinegar. You might want to wear gloves as they will release a bit of juice.

Put the walnuts in the brine. Cover with an old tea towel and leave for 7 days out of direct sunlight. The water will soon resemble an oil slick and the walnuts near the top will start to turn black; this is due to them being exposed to oxygen.

After 3 days turn them over so that the undersides get a turn at the top. Then, after 7 days it's time to re-brine. Drain, rinse and then repeat the process.

After 14 days, drain and rinse the walnuts again. Pat dry and then place on a windowsill until they have all turned black, this will take a day or two depending on the weather. They will also shrink a little.

Combine the wine, vinegars, sugar and spices in a pan. Bring to boiling point then simmer for 30 mins. Allow to cool to hand hot. Place the walnuts into sterilised jars and cover with the liquid ensuring that all the spices are evenly distributed.

Seal the jars and place in a cool dark place to mature. This takes about 6 months.

Green walnut nocino

This recipe came to me around 12 years ago from Gilly Wright, who was living in Italy at the time. It also uses green walnuts.

Ingredients

29 green walnuts
2 cinnamon sticks
2 thumbs of wood avens root or 5 cloves
1 sprig of spruce, 10 pine needles or the zest of 1 lemon
500g/1lb 2oz sugar
1 litre/1¾ pints vodka or grappa

Method

Rinse and pat dry the walnuts. Cut into quarters.

Place all the dry ingredients into the jar along with the walnuts. Top up with the booze.

Place in a cool, dark place and shake daily for the first week or so to help dissolve the sugar. After 7 days, only shake twice a week for a couple of months.

After 2 months, strain the liquid into bottles and leave it for 6 months to a year. I know that seems like a long time, but believe me, you'll be glad you did. Immature nocino is rather bitter and it will mellow with age.

Wild garlic

Allium ursinum

After blackberries, apples and perhaps plums, wild garlic, with its distinctive scent, is one of the few plants that most people can forage without fear in the UK.

Wild garlic grows from a bulb just like its cultivated cousin, and spear-shaped leaves start to grow from the bulb during late winter. The bulb should be left alone, as it's illegal to harvest without the landowner's permission. It's also kinder to the plant, as this ensures it can regenerate next season.

Its leaves are green, and I mean really green. Unlike many other plants, you can find very young specimens alongside older ones. At the peak of the growing season in late winter (north) or early spring (south), lift up the leaves to find smaller leaves growing beneath. This is especially useful, as when the plants have started to flower the leaves can become tough and chewy.

The flowers themselves are white with six sharply pointed petals and grow on stalks protruding from a central stem. They tend to grow in little clusters of up to 25. As the season progresses, the flowers will turn into little round balls that contain the small seeds for the next generation.

AT A GLANCE

Where it grows

Broadleaf woodland; in dappled shade.

Brief description

Green, leafy plant; long leaves; white star-shaped flowers.

Lookalikes

Lily of the valley; lords-and-ladies.

Dangers

Both lookalikes are poisonous.

Conservation notes

Pick carefully and methodically to avoid picking anything else.

When to harvest

Grows Jan–May/June, but is best in March.

Use in

Young leaves sparingly in salads or for pesto; older leaves can be cooked; green seeds can be pickled.

Fun fact

Traces of allium pollen have been found at a Neolithic site in Switzerland, suggesting a long history of human consumption.

The smell is the plant's most distinguishing feature. Pick a leaf, crush it in your hand and take a big sniff. If it doesn't smell of garlic, then it's not wild garlic.

All parts of the plant are edible. I like to use the young leaves sparingly in a salad or as pesto. They can also be fermented but will need to be chopped small as the leaves can get caught in your throat. As the leaves get older and more fibrous they are much better finely chopped and then cooked. At this stage I prefer to pick just the stems, which I cut and use in place of spring or salad onions.

At the very end of the season, as the shade of trees restricts the sunlight for this opportunistic plant, there is still one last harvest to be had. The small round seed balls, which poke up on stems across the woodland floor, can be added to a coarse grain mustard. They can also be fermented and used like capers.

WILD GARLIC
Around 25 flowers form rounded clusters on single, leafless stalks.
Leaves are long and pointed with smooth edges.
Look for wild garlic in woodlands and hedgerows in early spring.

The poisonous lily of the valley (*Convallaria majalis*) has been cited as a lookalike by foragers. The leaves are the same shape and it also has white flowers. However, the leaves are much coarser, are a duller green and they don't smell, and its flowers are bell-shaped. Another poisonous species, lords-and-ladies (*Arum maculatum*) can grow in the same spot (see page 167).

Wild garlic pesto

The first time I made this pesto, I was expecting it to be as strong as shop-bought pesto. It was much more potent and took me a few days to recover! Use sparingly, and if you find the garlic a little overpowering, add a few other leaves to temper it: I suggest rocket, baby leaf spinach or sow thistle.

Ingredients

50g/$1\frac{3}{4}$oz cracked and peeled foraged hazelnuts or pine nuts
80g/$2\frac{3}{4}$oz/1 handful of wild garlic leaves
30g/1oz Parmesan cheese
150ml/5fl oz oil (hempseed/olive/cold pressed rapeseed)
A squeeze of lemon juice

Method

Toast the nuts in a pan until they are golden and the smell fills the kitchen. Put in a blender with all the other ingredients and blend until smooth.

The resulting pesto can then be stored in jars in the fridge for about a week or so. To ensure freshness, leave a little gap at the top of the jar and pour over a little of the oil to help seal the pesto beneath. To keep the pesto for longer, it can be stored in ice cube racks in the freezer.

Wild garlic mustard

There is something truly delicious about combining mustard and garlic. However, mustard seeds often come into season long after the wild garlic has died back. This means you either have to cheat a little and use shop-bought mustard seeds or keep some back from the previous season's harvest. Both yellow and black mustard seeds can be used in this recipe, but you are more likely to find black mustard seeds in the wild (as you are in the shops).

Ingredients

100g/3½oz wild (if possible) yellow or black mustard seeds
100g/3½oz wild garlic seeds
200ml/7fl oz raw apple cider vinegar
250ml/9fl oz filtered or unchlorinated water (see page 71)
15g/1 tablespoon sea salt

Method

Place all your ingredients into a jar and stir well. I like to use a wooden chopstick for stirring ferments like this one, as it helps to pinpoint the rogue mustard or garlic seeds that stick to the sides of the jar.

Although I like to steer clear of plastic at any given opportunity, I would also advise filling a zip-lock bag with water and placing that inside the jar, this helps to keep any very buoyant seeds below the water line. Anything above the water line may come into contact with airborne spores and could become mouldy.

Cover your jar with a small piece of material. Leave the jar in a cool, dark place for 3 days. Once fermented, you can transfer into smaller jars and give away as presents. Remember to keep refrigerated and use within a year or so.

WILD STRAWBERRY

Wild strawberries look like miniature versions of commercial varieties.

Wild strawberry

Fragaria vesca

Wild or alpine strawberries look like 'real' strawberries, only they are tiny and taste amazing; more so than any cultivated strawberry. Foraging for them can be frustrating as often you think you have found some only for it to be a barren strawberry plant (*Potentilla sterilis*). Worse still is the mock strawberry (*P. indica*), a dreadful cultivated plant that produces watery, tasteless, strawberry-like fruits.

You may dream of filling baskets, but the reality is that most of your foraging outings only ever furnish you with a handful of delicious fruits. It's better not to worry about abundance (the birds will thank you for being so considerate) and to appreciate the taste of each one as much as you did the first.

The plants can creep along the ground. In our garden, we've managed to cover a rather large flower bed with alpine strawberries. The runners or stolons hang down, in our case over 1 metre (3¼ feet) in length. Whenever they connect with soil, another plant starts to grow. Given the right conditions they

AT A GLANCE

Where they grow

Open and part-shaded woodlands; margins, scrub and banks that get at least 6 hours of sunlight. Likes alkaline soils and rock but grows in most soils.

Brief description

Like a regular strawberry, only smaller.

Lookalikes

Barren and mock strawberries.

Conservation notes

Always leave enough for the birds.

When to harvest

From the first day of Wimbledon onwards.

Use in

Eat raw.

Fun fact

The word 'strawberry' is derived from the Anglo-Saxon *streawberige*, or 'strewing berry', and most probably refers to the way the plant spreads across the ground.

will spread far and wide. However, they seem to cower given any competition, so are unlikely to take over.

The leaves come in groups of three (trifoliate), and are toothed and green like a regular strawberry leaf, only smaller. The five-petalled flowers are small and white. Each plant produces a succession of leaves and often you can see that cycle in action, with some leaves dying off, while others are folded in half beneath the vibrant, dominant leaves that are feeding the plant. The fruits are oblong and red, like tiny versions of regular cultivated strawberries.

I highly recommend picking as you go and enjoying each burst of flavour and each moment you get to taste it. If you do get enough for a pudding, keep it simple, perhaps serving with just a dollop of cream. Alternatively, you could crush a few strawberries, add a tiny pinch of salt, and a splash of white wine vinegar and oil to make a simple, fruity salad dressing.

Wood avens

herb bennet, clove root

Geum urbanum

Whatever you want to call this plant, it is most easily identified by digging it up (with permission) in the spring. Wash it and then scratch at the root. Have a big sniff and what do you smell? Cloves I hope, as this plant contains the essential oil eugenol, the main constituent of cloves.

It's a plant that initially likes to hang out on the margins, hidden away and not at all showy. Once it reaches maturity, it starts to show off a little. Its bright yellow flowers poke up out of the ground on long stems, later turning into ornate spiky balls with little red hooks that attach themselves to passing animals. Each flower has five petals and they appear across the summer.

The leaves are covered in a kind of downy hair and comprise 3–5 lobes. The whole plant can grow up to 60 centimetres (24 inches) high, although often it is much shorter. The roots are often a tangle of thin fibres growing from a fatter root at the top.

AT A GLANCE

Where they grow

Woodland edges; damp places.

Brief description

Straggly plant found in dark corners. Hated by many gardeners.

Lookalikes

Buttercups.

Dangers

Confusion with inedible buttercups. Avoid if pregnant or breastfeeding.

Conservation notes

Common but check if any insect has been nibbling at a plant you plan to uproot.

When to harvest

Spring.

Use in

The root has a mild clove flavour. The infused root makes a good chai with 1 teaspoon of dried magnolia.

Fun fact

Used as an early form of deodorant. Sewn into clothes, it would mask any bodily odours.

WOOD AVENS
The leaves comprise 3-5 lobes.
The root, which smells of clove, can be infused to make chai.
The roots are often a tangle of thin fibres.

Mulled apple juice

Every year, a week or two before Christmas, we have an open house for our friends and their families. Every guest gets offered a drink on arrival. We scour the local area for wild ingredients the night before and throw them all in our largest cooking pot.

The recipe below is non-alcoholic but will work equally well with wine, cider or dark ales such as porters and stouts. The ingredients can be varied according to taste and the quantities increased depending on how many people you are catering for. The trick to making any mulled drink is to keep tasting as you go along.

Due to *Phytophthora austrocedri* (*P. austrocedri*), an aggressive, fungus-like pathogen which infects juniper, its berries are increasingly rare in this country. Don't be ashamed to buy juniper for this recipe.

Ingredients

1 litre/2 pints apple juice
2 wood avens roots (washed)
4-5 juniper berries
1 large sprig of spruce tips or a fistful of pine needles
10 coriander seeds
1 star anise
1 cinnamon stick

Method

Put all the ingredients into your saucepan and heat until it is gently simmering. Stir and keep simmering for about 10 minutes. Taste a spoonful and ensure that you are happy with your flavour; remember, you can always add more or less of something if you are not.

Serve your mulled apple juice in china tea cups and don't forget the trick to good mulling is to simmer and not to boil.

Poisonous plants

When teaching foraging, I always start with a warning: there are plants out there that can and will make you very ill or even kill you – or members of your family. It is right to be faint-hearted about these plants. Even if you are the slightest bit unsure whether or not a plant is poisonous, then leave it alone. That instinct is what will keep you alive. That said, if you familiarise yourself with the enemies, you'll be able to pick out your friends when you come across them. Study the plants on the next few pages carefully, so you can rule them out definitively.

The entries are not an exhaustive list of all the poisonous plants in the UK – that is another book in itself – but they are some of the most common. They are also the plants you are most likely to confuse with the edible ones in this book. You still need to be cautious if you can't be sure that your edible plant isn't one of the following; for that I would also advise cross referencing with other books.

Foxglove

Digitalis purpurea

Looks like: Comfrey, primrose, burdock and dock

Ingestion of this plant causes heart and kidney problems. In the early stages of growth, the coarse leaves can be confused with comfrey. The edge of the comfrey leaf is smooth while the foxglove has a toothed edge. The foxglove is also very soft. Get to know them in flower and always double check if unsure.

In its first year the leaves grow in a rosette close to the ground. After the first year, foxgloves grow up to 2 metres (6½ feet) in height with alternate leaves growing up the stem. You'll find foxgloves growing next to hedges, on farmland, moorland, near beaches and planted in gardens.

The plants produce many bell-shaped purple flowers, which are often visited by bees.

FOXGLOVE
POISONOUS
The leaves can be confused with comfrey. Foxglove is downy and soft with wavy, toothed margins.
Bees bury themselves inside the bell-shaped flowers.

Hemlock

Conium maculatum

Looks like: Cow parsley, yarrow, wild carrot, angelica, wild parsnip, hogweed

Note the Latin name here as there is more than one hemlock plant, and both are poisonous, which shouldn't be much of a surprise. A biennial, the young plants grow in large rosettes close to the ground, while mature plants sometimes exceed 2 metres (6½ feet) in height. It will grow along verges, field and park edges on rewilding land, and close to streams and rivers.

The crushed leaves smell unpleasant; I liken it to the smell of mice. The stems are covered in purple blotches, which resemble the rash caused by rubella. As with the illness, the blotches can be minimal or extensive. When cut down the middle, the stems are hollow and round.

Its fern-like leaves are glossy and a rather vivid bright green; slightly feathery in appearance, they are more like parsley than fennel. The flowers are small and white and appear in umbrella-like clusters. They will appear from spring to summer and when the plant sets seed it will die off.

Check every source at your disposal if you have even the slightest suspicion that a plant could be hemlock. It must be ruled out every time.

HEMLOCK

POISONOUS

Leaves are glossy
and smell musty
when crushed.

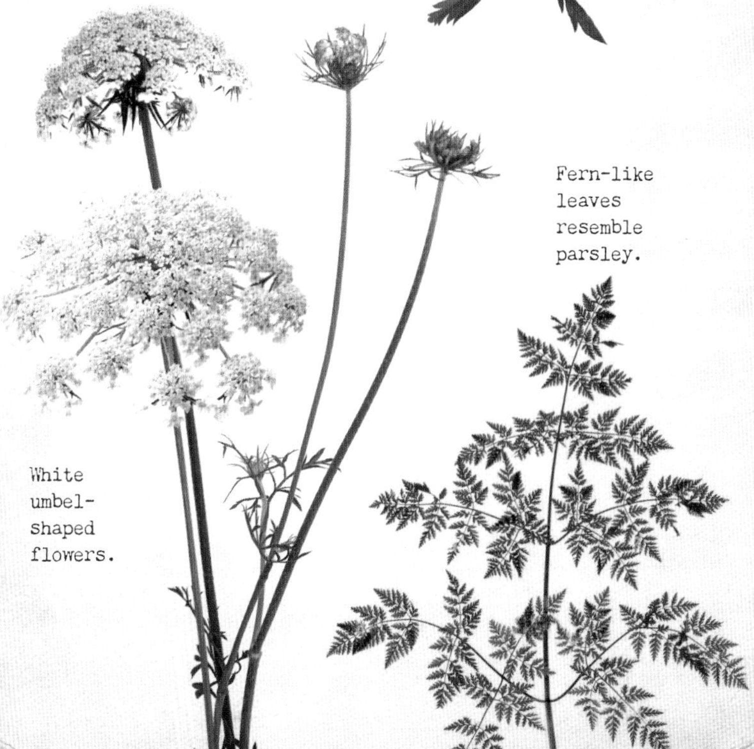

Fern-like
leaves
resemble
parsley.

White
umbel-
shaped
flowers.

Hemlock water-dropwort

Oenanthe crocata

Looks like: Cow parsley, yarrow, wild carrot, angelica, wild parsnip, fennel

I was once sent an email by someone asking if it was okay to forage a huge field of yarrow they had found. Yarrow is a feather-like herb with a white flower head shaped like an upside-down umbrella. What their photo actually showed was a field of hemlock water-dropwort, regarded as the deadliest plant in the UK.

A group of eight people camping in Argyll once mistakenly made a curry from the roots. By morning, one member of the group had suffered violent muscle contractions, hallucinations and a loss of consciousness, and was admitted to hospital. The other members of the group all suffered from varying degrees of nausea, vomiting, lethargy, sweating and fever. Four more had to go to hospital but all were later discharged. They were very lucky – it is estimated that up to 70 per cent of people who ingest this plant will die.

The trouble is that hemlock water-dropwort is common and it looks like so many tasty plants. Fennel, one of its many lookalikes, is included in this book, so please study the plant on this page and make sure you are not picking it. Hemlock water-dropwort is a plant that identification apps often get dangerously wrong. They might tell you it is parsnip or celery, for example, so don't trust apps when it comes to any plant in the carrot family.

HEMLOCK WATER-DROPWORT

POISONOUS

Can grow up to 1½ metres/5 feet high.

Clusters of white flowers are carried in umbels.

Leaves are similar to flat-leaf parsley.

It is a good indicator of water, very rarely growing more than 20 metres (66 feet) from a water source, so you will find it in damp areas, such as river edges, marshes, ditches and woodlands.

The plant is vividly green. The major difference between this and other umbellifers is that it is completely hairless. The stems are rounded and slightly flattened, they also have ridges down them. It often grows in abundance and it can be tall, up to 1.5 metres (5 feet). The flowers are carried in umbels (upside-down umbrellas) and contain clusters of white flowers. Smell is always a good indicator: it will be acrid and unpleasant, although I have heard some describe it as being like sweet parsley. The leaves do look a lot like flat leaf parsley, especially to the untrained eye.

Lords-and-ladies

cuckoo-pint

Arum maculatum

Looks like: Wild garlic

If you accidentally eat the leaf of a lords-and-ladies, you'll soon know it. It will start to burn the inside of your mouth, and if you keep on chewing your throat will seize up. If that doesn't kill you, the internal inflammation that follows will cause convulsions before death. Not the nicest way to go.

Its leaves could be mistaken for sorrel or perhaps wild garlic. They often appear just before wild garlic and the eager forager could easily pick some by mistake. As the season progresses, you might also find them beneath wild garlic leaves. This is another reason to pick wild garlic slowly and steadily.

Lords-and-ladies leaves are arrow-shaped, dark green and glossy, in the same way as ivy leaves. As they grow, they also become flecked with black spots – hence the Latin species name *maculatum* meaning 'spotted' or 'stained'. They can be easily confused with sorrel leaves, which is partly why I left sorrel out of this book. However, you'll note that sorrel leaves are sharply pointed and those of lords-and-ladies are more rounded. A friend of mine describes sorrel leaves as looking as if they have been 'cut with scissors'.

By springtime, the flowers will appear. They are rather strange-looking and stand out on the forest floor. You'll note the central part of the flower (the spadix) is club-shaped and will start off green and ripen to a deeper chocolate brown. This is surrounded by the protective covering or bract, which makes it looks as if the spadix is wearing a hood.

LORDS-AND-LADIES

POISONOUS

All parts of the plant, including the orange-red berries are poisonous.

These plants have strangely shaped flowers and arrow-shaped leaves.

Eventually, the plant will start to fruit. It produces little spikes of green and then orange-red berries poking out of the ground. These berries are also poisonous.

Monk's-hood

Wolfsbane

Aconitum spp.

Looks like: Mugwort, wormwood

The entire plant, tip to root, is extremely poisonous and can cause a severe reaction or death. Gardeners should be cautious and only handle with gloves. The leaves are made up of five to seven deeply divided lobes that are hairless and toothed. The hairless stems will reach up to 1 metre (3¼ feet) in height. The flowers, which resemble the hood of a monk (hence the common name), are mainly blue-purple, but garden cultivars can vary. These hooded menaces like to hang out in damp woodland and in ditches.

MONK'S-HOOD

POISONOUS

The stems can reach up to 1 metre in height.

The leaves are hairless and toothed.

The purple flowers have a distinctive hooded shape.

Ragwort

Jacobaea vulgaris

Looks like: Tansy, dandelion, St John's wort

This plant can also be confused with mugwort (see page 93). The poison in the plant gets to work on the liver causing irreversible cirrhosis. Some people mistakenly think it can kill horses, however, grazing animals will reject what is poisonous unless it is given to them as hay. We allow a small patch to grow in our back garden for the 77 insect species that thrive on it, including the cinnabar moth.

From July to October, expect to find yellow, daisy-like flowers sitting atop a plant that grows between 30 centimetres (12 inches) and 1 metre (3¼ feet) tall. The leaves are green and smooth, but can be a little hairy on the underside where they are also lighter.

RAGWORT

POISONOUS

Ragwort has lots of yellow, daisy-like flowers between July and October.

It provides food for the cinnabar moth.

Yew

Taxus baccata

Looks like: Spruce

It is thought our pagan ancestors planted yew trees on ground they believed to be sacred. These sites continued to be venerated following the introduction of Christianity and churches were often built on sites where some of our oldest yew trees still grow. In extreme old age, the yew's trunk often splits and you'll find many trunks arching close to the ground.

At the other end of the spectrum, youthful yews can be found dotted around the understorey of woodlands. To identify them, look at the needles, each will be 2–4 centimetres (1–1½ inches) in length, dark green with a grey-green underside, flattened, and most importantly will not have the fragrant 'pine' smell of a spruce. Avoid crushing yew leaves as they are toxic. Yews also carry red berries with poisonous seeds.

YEW
POISONOUS
Flat leaves line up either side of young shoots and spiral around older shoots.
The berries will help you identify a yew tree. The pips are very poisonous.

Further reading and resources

Books

Gunn, Emma, *Never Mind the Burdocks*, Bramble & Bean Publishing House (2018)

Johnson, Owen and David More, *Collins Tree Guide*, Collins (2006)

Hamilton, Andy, *Booze for Free*, Eden Project Books (2017)

Harford, Robin, *Edible and Medicinal Wild Plants of Britain and Ireland* (2019)

Harrap, Simon, *Harrap's Wild Flowers*, Bloomsbury (2018)

Irving, Miles, *The Forager Handbook*, Ebury Press (2009)

Mabey, Richard, *Food for Free*, Collins (1993)

Nozedar, Adele, *The Garden Forager*, Square Peg (2015)

Rensten, John, *The Edible City: A Year of Wild Food*, Boxtree (2016).

Rose, Francis, *The Wild Flower Key*, Warne (2006)

Streeter, David, *Collins Wild Flower Guide*, Collins (2016)

Wright, John, *The Forager's Calendar*, Profile Books (2020)

Walker, Kim and Vicky Chown, *The Handmade Apothecary: Healing herbal recipes*, Kyle Books (2018)

Courses and websites

Visit www.foragers-association.org/directory to find a forager near you who has been vetted and approved by other foragers. Also, you will find links to many of the members' websites and social media profiles – enough to keep you busy and up to date with the latest foraging advances.

Acknowledgements

Thanks first of all to Emma Wright, for proofing, tasting and for always asking before throwing away random things in jars. To my writers group, Corinne Dobinson, David Griffiths, Simon Leake, Mike Manson, Ray Newman, Piers Mater, Kate Sykes and Tony Taylor for all of your notes, edits and encouragement.

Huge thanks to everyone at the Association of Foragers for existing. Especially to those who offered direct advice or recipes – Alex McAllister-Lunt (Force of Nature Chef), Rob Gould (the Cotswold forager), Lisa Cutcliffe (Edulis Wild Food), Kim Walker, Adele Nozedar (Brecon Beacons Foraging), Sam Webster (Foraging Forages), Szymon Szyszczakiewicz (Foragerium), Jennie Martin, John Rensten (Forage London) David Winnard (Discover the Wild) and Mark Williams (Galloway Wild Foods) and Joanna Ruminska (Incredible Edible).

Also to Peter Taylor my editor for being the right mix of laid-back and enthusiastic for a project to run smoothly and Katie Hewett and Clare Savage for their final editing. Everyone at Harper Collins and especially David Salmo, and also Claire Masset and Emily Roe from the National Trust. My agent Kate Johnson for her yogic agenting. Also, to each person who helped design, ship, pack, print, typeset, market, along with all the other people who do the unseen jobs to help create a book. Lastly and (in advance) to all of the volunteers and workers in every bookshop and gift shop that will sell this book. Without you all, a writer is nothing but an ego on a keyboard.

But thanks must also go to the other foragers I've met, the ones who inspire with their enthusiasm and love of all things wild. They include, John Wright, Craig Worrall (Edible Leeds), Emma Gunn, Martin Bailey, Daniel Butler, Nicola Jay Burgess, Lizzy Mary-Jane Farmer, Richard Mawby, Ru Kenyon, Stuart Hippach, Graham Whitehouse, Miles Irving, Freya Rimington Fergus Drennan, Tizane Reeves, Robin Harford, Łukasz Łuczaj, Gemma Hindi, Fred Gillam, Amanda Montague, Francois Couplan, Mo Wilde, Courtney Tyler, Heather Thomas-Smith, Jim Parums, Clothilde Walenne, Bill O'Dea, Rachel Lambert, Zaneta Wright, Christine Westgate, Christine Whitehouse, Leanne Townsend, Brian Hoey, Susanne Masters, Christy Miles, Matthew Rooney, Julia Behrens, Vicky Manning, Amy Rankine, Vivienne Campbell, Neville Kilkenny, Julia and Matthew Bruton-Seal, Daniel Evans-Pughe, Rupert Waites, Tom Martin-Wells, Michael Webber, Sarah Watson, Colin Wheeler-James, Mina Said-Allsopp and the Michael White. I've learned so much more off you guys than could ever be taught in a university. Hey, remember last time I had an idea and I left you all to set up the Association of Foragers; who wants to set up the IOF, the Institute of Foraging?

Index

All images are courtesy of Shutterstock except for the following: Alamy: 7. Getty Images: 45. Andy Hamilton: 129. National Trust Images/Annapurna Mellor: 17, 118, 148. National Trust Images/Stephen Robson: 20. National Trust Images/Harry Davies: 27. National Trust Images/Jemma Finch: 60. National Trust Images/James Dobson: 88.